HAZEL'S HYMNS

by

Hazel Bradley

This book is dedicated to the memory of Sandy Macpherson,
a kind and generous man in whose company I spent
many happy childhood years.

Hazel's Hymns
© Hazel Bradley 1993

ISBN 1 85852 011 8

All rights reserved. No part of this publication may be reproduced, stored in a retrieval system, transmitted, in any form or by any means, electronic, mechanical, photocopying, recording or otherwise, without the prior permission of Foundery Press, 20 Ivatt Way, Peterborough PE3 7PG.

Printed in England by Clays Ltd, St Ives plc

CONTENTS

	Page
Introduction	4
Abide with me	6
All things bright and beautiful	8
Amazing grace	10
And can it be	12
At the name of Jesus	14
Christians, awake	16
Come, ye thankful people, come	18
Crown him with many crowns	20
Dear Lord and Father of mankind	22
Eternal Father	24
For all the saints	26
Guide me, O thou great Jehovah	28
Hark the glad sound!	30
Holy, holy, holy	32
How great thou art	34
In Christ there is no east or west	36
In the bleak mid-winter	38
It came upon the midnight clear	40
It is God who holds the nations	42
Lead us, heavenly Father, lead us	44
Mine eyes have seen the glory	46
Nearer, my God, to thee	48
O come, O come, Immanuel	50
O God, our help in ages past	52
O Jesus, I have promised	54
Onward, Christian soldiers	56
O worship the King, all-glorious above	60

	Page
Rock of Ages	62
Still the night	64
Tell me the old, old story	66
The church's one foundation	68
The day thou gavest	70
The King of love	72
Thou whose almighty word	74
To God be the glory	76
Turn back, O man	78
We plough the fields	80
What a friend we have in Jesus	82
When the roll is called up yonder	84
When we walk with the Lord	86
While shepherds watched	88
Whosoever heareth! Shout, shout the sound	90
Who would true valour see	92
Index of Authors	94

Hazel Bradley

INTRODUCTION

I was just twelve years old when I first stood in front of a BBC microphone to audition for the Sunday morning radio programme 'Chapel in the Valley'. For many families in the 1950s and 60s the familiar signature tune and the gentle voice of Sandy Macpherson introducing the hymns and songs was the right kind of beginning to their Sunday. The 'Chapel' became a real place for them, although of course the programme was actually recorded in a studio.

I am amazed at how many people still remember Mr Edwards singing such favourites as 'The Blind Ploughman', Mr Drewett playing over the organ voluntary and the little girl from the Sunday School practising the children's hymns in readiness for the morning service. First Marion, then Anne (surnames were never used in the early days) were introduced to the listeners and then came Hazel, who stayed in the 'Chapel' as the little girl for ten years!

It is a period of my life that I look back on with great fondness. Sandy, his wife Florence and his secretary Joyce Hepple were like a second family to me as we travelled around the country taking part in concerts, organ recitals and other church money-raising events. It sometimes looked and felt as if my schooling and subsequent teacher training were fitted in around all these other activities but somehow I managed to come out with reasonable results, despite the reservations of some of my tutors.

I still have many of the letters that were written to me, often by people who had been touched by the words of a particular hymn. A verse or even just a line may have brought them comfort or hope or reminded them of days gone by, and as I read of their experience I began to realise what a profound influence a hymn can have on a person's life. Some struck up a correspondence which lasted through many series, sending me embroidered hankies when I had a cold, and one elderly gentleman sent me a handwritten text every month. I remember shedding more than a few tears when they stopped coming.

'Chapel in the Valley', with its simple gospel hymns and songs, seemed to reach the hearts of so many and when in 1970, as a result of Sandy Macpherson's failing health it came to an end, the programme was sadly missed. Indeed, people still say to me that their Sunday mornings have never been the same since the 'Chapel in the Valley' closed its doors. Quite a few years elapsed before I once again entered the doors of the BBC and during that time I married, moved to Warrington, produced two children, became a Methodist Local Preacher and when family permitted taught Religious Studies at the local high school.

This time, however, it was my speaking voice that was requested by Graham Carter, the producer of 'Daybreak', BBC Radio Merseyside's religious magazine programme, and I was asked to record some 'Thoughts for the Day'. Very soon I found myself a regular presenter and very much part of the team that put together a lively and topical Sunday programme. Graham was always looking for new items and when I suggested writing a weekly piece on the background of some of our favourite hymns, he was more than willing to give it a go. After a few weeks Peter Henegan, another member of the 'Daybreak' team, began to call it 'Hazel's Hymn' and the name stuck.

Listeners began to write in with their favourites, and what started as a group of five hymns and their stories developed into a series of twenty-two in 1990, followed in 1991 by a second set. A third series is in the pipeline as there are still many favourites that have not been included as yet. I wonder what YOUR choice would be?

Hazel Bradley

ABIDE WITH ME
Henry Francis Lyte, 1793-1847

Abide with me; fast falls the eventide;
The darkness deepens; Lord, with me abide;
    When other helpers fail, and comforts flee,
    Help of the helpless, O abide with me.

Swift to its close ebbs out life's little day;
Earth's joys grow dim, its glories pass away;
    Change and decay in all around I see;
    O thou who changest not, abide with me!

I need thy presence every passing hour;
What but thy grace can foil the tempter's power?
    Who like thyself my guide and stay can be?
    Through cloud and sunshine, O abide with me.

I fear no foe, with thee at hand to bless;
Ills have no weight, and tears no bitterness;
    Where is death's sting? Where, grave, thy victory?
    I triumph still, if thou abide with me.

Hold thou thy cross before my closing eyes;
Shine through the gloom, and point me to the skies;
    Heaven's morning breaks, and earth's vain shadows flee;
    In life, in death, O Lord, abide with me!

It is sung on Remembrance Sunday and at the Cup Final. It is a popular choice for funerals and has been used to bring many a Sunday evening service to a close. Surely 'Abide with me' must be a contender for Britain's all-time favourite hymn. We've been singing it for one hundred and forty-three years and yet it took only one hour to complete!

The writer was Henry Francis Lyte, born in 1793 near Kelso in Scotland, the son of an Army Officer. Educated in Enniskillen, he was the brightest boy in the school, a little eccentric, but popular with both staff and pupils. From there he went to Trinity College, Dublin to take up medicine but changed his course to read for Holy Orders. It was then that he developed a love of literature, especially poetry, and after his ordination to County Wexford, he began to lay the foundations for what was to become a large library.

After moving to Cornwall for health reasons, possibly tuberculosis, he married Anne Maxwell, an heiress, and eventually settled in the newly created parish of Lower Brixham.

On one occasion the townspeople became very excited as King William IV had been sighted in the royal yacht sailing into Tor Bay. Immediately the locals arranged for him to stand on the very spot in Brixham harbour on which William III had claimed the throne, and the assembled Church choir gave him a musical welcome. The King was so impressed that he gave Henry Lyte Berry House, a property far superior to the one he was then living in. It was here that he continued his writing and established a fine library, which included a rare collection of the books of Bishop Ken. Of course his wife's money made it all possible, but it was not a bottomless pit, and when it ran out in the 1830s, Henry Lyte had to take on pupils, one of whom became Lord Salisbury, Prime Minister under Queen Victoria no less than three times.

Throughout his life the Reverend Lyte was respected and loved by his parishioners, and many spoke highly of his devotion to duty in spite of failing health, but in 1847, sensing that the end was near, he preached his last sermon and said farewell to his flock of hardy fisher folk. He returned home to muse on the past and the future, and as he contemplated he wrote:

> 'Swift to its close ebbs out life's little day'

Completing the hymn, he entrusted it to his wife, and when the news of his death reached Brixham a few weeks later, his parishioners sang the now well-loved words for the first time in the Parish Church.

Since then the hymn has become a favourite at funerals, but I hope that it is not so locked into the genre that we feel it cannot be used on any other occasion. In 'Hymns and Psalms' it has been placed in the Faith and Confidence section alongside the Wesleys' birthday hymn 'Away with our fears', which seems to me to be a most appropriate neighbour.

ALL THINGS BRIGHT AND BEAUTIFUL
Cecil Frances Alexander, 1818-1895

All things bright and beautiful,
   All creatures great and small,
All things wise and wonderful,
   The Lord God made them all.

Each little flower that opens,
   Each little bird that sings,
He made their glowing colours,
   He made their tiny wings:

The purple-headed mountain,
   The river running by,
The sunset, and the morning
   That brightens up the sky:

The cold wind in the winter,
   The pleasant summer sun,
The ripe fruits in the garden,
   He made them every one:

He gave us eyes to see them,
   And lips that we might tell
How great is God Almighty,
   Who has made all things well:

Do you remember the old Sunday School Anniversary?

It was that special Sunday in the year when the children dressed up in their new clothes and stood impatiently while mother pinned a buttonhole on to the collar or lapel. The staging was set up so that every scholar could be seen singing or reciting the pieces they had been rehearsing for months. Every hymn was one that had been chosen with the children in mind, and a popular choice was that old favourite, 'All things bright and beautiful'.

Its author was born into a military family living in Dublin in 1818, and although her father's roots were in Norfolk, Major John Humphreys had become very much part of the Anglo-Irish gentry, working as Agent for the Wicklow estates. In fact, this second daughter was named after Lady Wicklow, and christened Cecil Frances.

Young Fanny, as she was called by her family, loved to write, and even as a small child it was clear that she was fascinated by words. At one point her family thought her too studious for a girl, and tried to guide her into other interests, but to no avail. Fanny continued to write her stories and poems.

When she was eleven the family moved nearer to the principal seat of the estate, Shelton Abbey. It was a beautiful place in which to grow up, surrounded by meadows and woods and only six miles from the coast. There were visits to her aunt in Scotland, where she met people like the poet Agnes Strickland who encouraged her talent.

The next move for Fanny was to County Tyrone, and it was here that many of her best loved hymns were written, as well as some tracts inspired by the Catholic revival. She met Doctors Pusey and Manning, and John Keble wrote the Preface to her celebrated 'Hymns for Little Children', published in 1848. This was her finest work with fourteen hymns specifically written to explain phrases from the Apostle's Creed in simple language. 'All things bright and beautiful' is one of these, illustrating 'I believe in God the Father Almighty, Maker of Heaven and Earth', and Fanny wrote it in the grounds of Markree Castle on the Ushwin River in Sligo. It was a huge house that had been renovated in Gothic style, and as she stood on the terrace she would have seen the 'river running by', the 'ripe fruits in the garden', and the 'tall trees in the greenwood', God's handiwork in the beauty of nature.

Frances Humphreys became Frances Alexander in 1850 and her husband later became Primate of All Ireland, but she will always be remembered for giving us such wonderful hymns as 'Once in Royal David's City', 'There is a green hill far away', and of course, 'All things bright and beautiful'.

AMAZING GRACE
John Newton, 1725-1807

Amazing grace (how sweet the sound)
    That saved a wretch like me!
I once was lost, but now am found,
    Was blind, but now I see.

Through many dangers, toils and snares
    I have already come;
God's grace has brought me safe thus far,
    And he will lead me home.

The Lord has promised good to me,
    His word my hope secures;
He will my shield and portion be
    As long as life endures.

And, when this heart and flesh shall fail
    And mortal life shall cease,
I shall possess within the veil
    A life of joy and peace.

How could there possibly be a link between an eighteenth century slave trader and an ecumenical Christian centre in Buckinghamshire? Well, there's a clue in the hymn 'How sweet the name of Jesus sounds in a believer's ear', and yet the comforting words are in such stark contrast to the early life-style of the author that it's almost impossible to believe that he could have written them.

John Newton was a shipmaster's son, and on his eleventh birthday was sent to sea against his will. He hated every minute of it, and by the time he was seventeen he had turned into the kind of son a father could be very ashamed of. His blasphemous language was such that even his ship-mates shuddered.

His father found a job for him in the West Indies managing a sugar plantation but John was busy chasing a girl in Chatham and missed the boat. But the press-gang didn't miss John Newton and he was forced to work under indescribable conditions until once again father came to the rescue and, in some sort of deal, managed to get his son a midshipman's post. Not that John was grateful. The thought of young Mary in Chatham got the better of him and he deserted. Freedom, however, was only to be for a few hours and his punishment was severe. He was publicly flogged and stripped of his rank.

Eventually John managed to get work on a slave ship bound for the African coast, but as usual fell foul of the captain and ended up receiving worse treatment than many of the slaves. The only thoughts that kept him going were of Mary from Chatham who, of course, had been forbidden to write to him. During one particularly bad storm he came across a copy of 'The Imitation of Christ' by Thomas a Kempis and the transformation began.

How his father managed to rescue him yet again is a story in itself, and what's more he married his beloved Mary, moved to Liverpool and became the Tide Surveyor. And it was here where he met John Wesley and the transformation became complete.

No-one was ever the same after meeting the great itinerant preacher, and the blaspheming sea-dog began to study the Christian faith. In 1764 he was ordained and appointed curate of Olney, Buckinghamshire. He began to write hymns, and with his great friend the poet William Cowper, produced a book entitled 'Olney Hymns' of which 'Amazing Grace' is perhaps the most well known.

Today a special trust has been formed in Olney, supported by all the churches there. The old vicarage has been turned into a Christian Centre and in the study above the fireplace there are two texts. So when you next sing the hymn 'Amazing Grace', imagine that 18th century sailor-cum-cleric looking up at them:

> 'Since thou art turned to the Lord, thou art honourable
> But thou must remember thou was a slave in Egypt.'

The change had been truly astonishing.

AND CAN IT BE
Charles Wesley, 1707-1788

And can it be that I should gain
    An interest in the Saviour's blood?
Died he for me, who caused his pain?
    For me, who him to death pursued?
Amazing love! How can it be
That thou, my God, shouldst die for me?

'Tis mystery all: the Immortal dies!
    Who can explore his strange design?
In vain the first-born seraph tries
    To sound the depths of love divine.
'Tis mercy all!   Let earth adore,
Let angel minds enquire no more.

He left his Father's throne above –
    So free, so infinite his grace –
Emptied himself of all but love,
    And bled for Adam's helpless race.
'Tis mercy all, immense and free;
For, O my God, it found out me!

Long my imprisoned spirit lay
    Fast bound in sin and nature's night;
Thine eye diffused a quickening ray –
    I woke, the dungeon flamed with light,
My chains fell off, my heart was free,
I rose, went forth, and followed thee.

No condemnation now I dread;
    Jesus and all in him, is mine!
Alive in him, my living Head,
    And clothed in righteousness divine,
Bold I approach the eternal throne,
And claim the crown, through Christ, my own.

I have to admit that I would find it very difficult to choose just one hymn by Charles Wesley, as there are so many favourites among the six thousand that he wrote. How he managed to find the time in his action-packed life to put pen to paper on so many occasions never ceases to amaze me.

Charles Wesley came from a large family where life was never dull. His father, an unpopular Lincolnshire parson, was mobbed by his parishoners when he voted Tory, imprisoned in Lincoln Gaol for non-payment of a debt, and his Rectory seemed to be under constant attack from those who supported Dissent.

Even within the Wesley home there were disagreements. Mrs Wesley refused to say 'Amen' when her husband prayed for King William III. Despite her husband's threat to deny her conjugal rights, she managed to produce nineteen children, of whom Charles was the eighteenth.

When he went to Westminster School his eldest brother Samuel was on the staff and paid his fees, and it was a good investment, as Charles went on to Oxford and was ordained in 1735. Three years later he was converted, and the hymnwriting and the evangelistic missions began in earnest. He was particularly good with prisoners and accompanied many to the scaffold.

In between all this activity he did find time to court the young Sarah Gwynne, twenty years his junior, and although her mother and brother took a lot of persuading on account of Charles' lack of finance, the family eventually gave their blessing, and his 'faithful Sally' as he called her, could often be seen riding pillion on his horse as they travelled the countryside together. Only three of their eight children survived, but the two boys went on to distinguished careers in music. If I was forced to make a choice of just one of his hymns, I think it would be 'And can it be that I should gain an interest in the Saviour's blood?'.

Perhaps you have been part of a large congregation singing these words with great gusto to Thomas Campbell's wonderful tune 'Sagina', and as the hymn builds up into a crescendo at the end of each verse and the voices divide there are often more than a few misty eyes and wobbling bottom lips. It is a very powerful hymn and many see it as the Wesley's conversion hymn rather than, 'Where shall my wandering soul begin?' We know that both hymns were written only a matter of hours after Charles had made the 'great change' as he called it, and possibly his brother John sang it on the eve of his own conversion three days later.

'And can it be' is still very popular with young people. Only recently I was present at the confirmation of a group of teenagers who had specifically requested that this hymn be sung at the service. The range of theology that Charles Wesley manages to fit into the six verses displays his unique skill, although only five verses are printed in most of our hymnbooks. I think that is probably a blessing, as some of us are already running out of breath by verse four!

AT THE NAME OF JESUS
Caroline Maria Noel, 1817-1877

At the name of Jesus
   Every knee shall bow,
Every tongue confess him
   King of Glory now.
'Tis the Father's pleasure
   We should call him Lord,
Who from the beginning
   Was the mighty Word.

Humbled for a season,
   To receive a name
From the lips of sinners
   Unto whom he came,
Faithfully he bore it
   Spotless to the last,
Brought it back victorious
   When from death he passed:

Bore it up triumphant
   With its human light,
Through all ranks of creatures
   To the central height,
To the throne of Godhead,
   To the Father's breast;
Filled it with the glory
   Of that perfect rest.

In your hearts enthrone him;
   There let him subdue
All that is not holy,
   All that is not true;
Crown him as your captain
   In temptation's hour:
Let his will enfold you
   In its light and power.

For this same Lord Jesus
   Shall return again,
With his Father's glory,
   With his angel train;
All the wreaths of empire
   Meet upon his brow,
And our hearts confess him
   King of Glory now.

The more I look into the background of our well-loved hymns the more I find out how many editors have tried to alter them. There are many examples in 'Hymns Ancient and Modern' where the hymns have been 'improved upon', often to the annoyance of the author. You may have noticed, for instance, that in some hymnbooks the first line of 'At the name of Jesus' reads 'In the name of Jesus' which could lead to problems if you were looking it up in the index. In the Methodist 'Hymns & Psalms' it is sensibly listed under both. But how did the problem arise in the first place?

It seems that the original wording used 'at', because the hymn is based on a passage from Philippians 2 which reads, in the King James version, 'that at the name of Jesus every knee should bow'. When the Revised Version of the Bible came out in 1881 the verse read 'in the name of Jesus', and, obviously carried away with the excitement of the new translation, the editors of a new hymnbook, 'Church Hymns', asked the family of the author for permission to change the first word. However, in subsequent translations, the authors reverted to 'at' again.

The author of 'At the name of Jesus' was Caroline Maria Noel, born in 1817 into the family of an evangelical Anglican Canon, Gerard Thomas Noel, living in Kent. Her uncle, the Honourable Baptist Wriothesley Noel, chaplain to Queen Victoria, had caused quite a stir by suddenly becoming a believer in baptism by total immersion and promptly joining the Baptist Church. Both men were hymnwriters so perhaps it seemed quite natural for young Caroline to pick up her pen.

She wrote her first hymn at the age of seventeen, and whether it was because of something that was said or her own dissatisfaction we don't know, but she didn't write another word until she was forty!

It looks as though it was her own illness at that time which re-kindled her interest, because she felt she wanted to write hymns that would comfort those who were suffering pain. She suffered considerable distress herself for the next twenty years but eventually put all her hymns into a book entitled 'The name of Jesus and other verses for the sick and lonely'. It seems that this hymn was a favourite from the very beginning – even a selling point.

Tunes can very often be a bone of contention, and 'At the name of Jesus' has at least five. The chances that I will choose the 'right' one for a given church service are pretty slim!

CHRISTIANS, AWAKE
John Byrom, 1692-1763

Christians, awake, salute the happy morn
Whereon the Saviour of the world was born;
Rise to adore the mystery of love,
Which hosts of angels chanted from above;
With them the joyful tidings first begun
Of God incarnate and the Virgin's Son.

Then to the watchful shepherds it was told,
Who heard the angelic herald's voice, 'Behold,
I bring good tidings of a Saviour's birth
To you and all the nations upon earth;
This day has God fulfilled his promised word,
This day is born a Saviour, Christ the Lord.'

He spake; and straightway the celestial choir
In hymns of joy, unknown before, conspire.
The praises of redeeming love they sang,
And heaven's whole orb with alleluias rang;
God's highest glory was their anthem still,
Peace upon earth, and unto men goodwill.

To Bethlem straight the enlightened shepherds ran,
To see the wonder God had wrought for man;
Then to their flocks, still praising God, return,
And their glad hearts with holy rapture burn;
Amazed, the wondrous tidings they proclaim,
The first apostles of his infant fame.

Like Mary, let us ponder in our mind
God's wondrous love in saving lost mankind;
Trace we the Babe, who has retrieved our loss,
From his poor manger to his bitter cross;
Tread in his steps, assisted by his grace,
Till our first heavenly state again takes place.

Then may we hope, the angelic hosts among,
To sing, redeemed, a glad triumphal song;
He that was born upon this joyful day
Around us all his glory shall display;
Saved by his love, incessant we shall sing
Th' eternal praise of heaven's almighty King.

He was the sort of man you couldn't ignore. Tall, striking appearance, and a bit of a 'snazzy' dresser. Dr John Byrom of Stockport was a contributor to the 'Spectator', inventor of a shorthand system and, of course, author of a very popular Christmas carol.

He was on coffee drinking terms with John and Charles Wesley, and met them to discuss the great theological questions, but he made his living by teaching his shorthand to all the literary people who wanted to take advantage of this marvellous time-saver. Apparently it was his system on which the famous Pitman shorthand course was based: just another of the fascinating facts one comes across when studying the history of hymns!

But it wasn't all work for John Byrom. He was a great family man and his daughter Dorothy was the apple of his eye. As Christmas approached in 1749 he asked his 'Dolly', as he called her, what she would like for her present, and no doubt he was rather surprised when his eleven year old daughter asked for a poem. An original of course, written by her father. And so when Christmas Day came and Dorothy ran to the breakfast table she discovered an envelope on her plate. Carefully opening it, she pulled out the paper and with great delight read out the poem written especially for her.

> 'Christians, awake, salute the happy morn
> Whereon the Saviour of the world was born.'

Dorothy must have been very proud of her gift as it soon became well known in the locality. John Wainwright, the organist of Stockport Parish Church, composed a tune for it, and the following Christmas there was another surprise, this time for the whole Byrom family. At precisely one minute after midnight on Christmas morning they all awoke to the sound of a choir beneath their window. Dorothy's poem had become a carol. It must have been a very special moment, and since then Christians have been re-living that moment in their Christmas Eve services in choosing this carol to usher in the special day.

It's a service that I'm particularly fond of, as by 11.30pm the turkey is stuffed and the last minute presents have been wrapped, and I can sit quietly and yet joyfully in a church packed with family and friends, all of us waiting to welcome the Christ child. As the minister lights the white candle in the centre of the Advent Ring we know that Christmas Day has finally dawned. The organ starts to play, and 'Christians awake' rings round the building: a child's gift which has been shared for over two hundred years.

COME, YE THANKFUL PEOPLE, COME
Henry Alford, 1810-1871

Come, ye thankful people, come,
Raise the song of harvest-home!
All is safely gathered in,
Ere the winter storms begin;
God, our maker, doth provide
For our wants to be supplied;
Come to God's own temple, come,
Raise the song of harvest-home!

All the world is God's own field,
Fruit unto his praise to yield;
Wheat and tares together sown,
Unto joy or sorrow grown;
First the blade, and then the ear,
Then the full corn shall appear;
Lord of harvest, grant that we
Wholesome grain and pure may be.

For the Lord our God shall come,
And shall take his harvest home;
From his field shall in that day
All offences purge away;
Give his angels charge at last
In the fire the tares to cast,
But the fruitful ears to store
In his garner evermore.

Even so, Lord, quickly come;
Bring thy final harvest home;
Gather thou thy people in,
Free from sorrow, free from sin,
There for ever purified,
In thy garner to abide:
Come, with all thine angels come,
Raise the glorious harvest home!

In the season of 'mists and mellow fruitfulness' no Harvest Festival worth its fruit and vegetables would be complete without the hymn, 'Come, ye thankful people come, raise the song of harvest-home.'

What memories it conjures up. Mouth-watering grapes hanging from the pulpit, enormous marrows on the communion rail, the children processing to the front with decorated baskets, and of course the plaited loaf in pride of place.

'First the blade and then the ear, then the full corn shall appear.' I wonder how many times those words are sung during the Autumn months, and yet it is only the first verse that takes the theme of harvest thanksgiving. The rest are on the subject of the last judgement, a mini-sermon in fact, which isn't surprising as the hymn's author, Henry Alford, was an outstanding preacher.

Imagine being born into a family where your father, grandfather, and so on, as far back as your great-great-great-grandfather had all been clergymen. Don't you think you may have felt under an obligation to take Holy Orders yourself?

Whether or not young Henry felt under any kind of pressure, he didn't disappoint his parents, becoming the vicar of a Leicestershire parish in 1835. It turned out to be extremely hard work, as his church was in a state of disrepair both physically and spiritually, but he set about his uphill task with seemingly boundless energy. Henry Alford was a positive inspiration to his congregation, building up both the faith and the fabric of the Church. He was a fund-raiser extraordinaire. Three thousand, five hundred pounds would be quite an achievement today, but to raise such a sum at the beginning of the nineteenth century was phenomenal. How he also managed to start a Greek New Testament and a History of the Jews, I don't know, but his obvious talent did not go unnoticed in high places, and it was Lord Palmerston who offered him the office of Dean of Canterbury.

Here he could work in peace, but he still liked to be involved in everything that was going on, and there's a lovely story linked with one of his other famous hymns, 'Forward be our watchword'. He had written the tune as well, but had added only the bass line, and when he gave it to the precentor of the Cathedral he wrote, "I have put it into its hat and boots, you can add the coat and trousers!" So we must add a sense of humour to his long list of attributes.

'Come, ye thankful people, come' was written while he was in Leicestershire and was published in his own book, 'Psalms and Hymns', in 1844. It was changed considerably when the editors of 'Hymns Ancient and Modern' got hold of it, which made Henry Alford furious because it was already very popular as it was. People tend to stick to what they like, and so the version we sing these days is very close to the original.

Henry Alford was only sixty when he was finally 'gathered in' but his hymns live on and bear witness to surely one of God's truly fruitful ears.

CROWN HIM WITH MANY CROWNS
Matthew Bridges, 1800-1894
Godfrey Thring, 1823-1903

Crown him with many crowns,
    The Lamb upon his throne;
Hark! How the heavenly anthem drowns
    All music but its own.
Awake, my soul, and sing
    Of him who died for thee,
And hail him as thy matchless King
    Through all eternity.

Crown him the Son of God,
    Before the worlds began;
And ye, who tread where he has trod,
    Crown him the Son of Man,
Who every grief has known
    That wrings the human breast,
And takes and bears them for his own,
    That all in him may rest.

Crown him the Lord of life,
    Who triumphed o'er the grave,
And rose victorious in the strife
    For those he came to save.
His glories now we sing,
    Who died, and rose on high;
Who died, eternal life to bring,
    And lives, that death may die.

Crown him the Lord of peace,
    Whose power a sceptre sways
From pole to pole, that wars may cease,
    Absorbed in prayer and praise.
His reign shall know no end,
    And round his piercèd feet
Fair flowers of paradise extend
    Their fragrance ever sweet.

Crown him the Lord of love;
    Behold his hands and side –
Rich wounds, yet visible above,
    In beauty glorified.
All hail, Redeemer, hail!
    For thou hast died for me;
Thy praise and glory shall not fail
    Throughout eternity.

I'm sure you will be familiar with such musical duos as Gilbert and Sullivan, Rodgers and Hammerstein, Lloyd Webber and Rice, but have you come across Bridges and Thring?

They were quite a different double act, not just because they were hymnwriters, but unlike the others who worked together, this pair never even met. Yet the hymn 'Crown him with many crowns' is attributed to them both. It's a case of what I call 'mix and match'.

It's a magnificent hymn which centres around the triumph of Jesus and hails him as King. It is a hymn that always comes to my mind as I stand in Liverpool's Metropolitan Cathedral of Christ the King, looking up at that beautiful lantern tower with its crown so easily picked out on the city skyline. Strangely enough Matthew Bridges, the man who wrote the original hymn in 1851, was originally an Anglican but later joined the Roman Catholic Church, and although English born spent most of his years in Canada. Perhaps it was while he was abroad that a certain Reverend Hutton, who had taken a fancy to most of the hymn, asked another author, Godfrey Thring, to write some more verses to replace those he felt rather weak, and so what we've ended up with is a kind of hybrid.

Gone are 'Crown him the Virgin's son' with reference to the 'mystic rose'. No more do we sing 'Crown him the Lord of years' with its rolling spheres and everlasting waves. Instead we have Rector Thring's verses starting 'Crown him the Son of God' and 'Crown him the Lord of life'. What Mr Bridges thought of this amalgam when he returned to England to visit the Convent of the Assumption in Sidmouth, I've not been able to find out, but I do know he never returned to Canada!

How often we sing these hymns Sunday after Sunday with no idea of the politics and events that surround them. Perhaps it's an advantage, as we can at least concentrate on the content, and this particular hymn, whichever version you have in your hymnbook, reminds us of the life and work of Jesus. It tells of him bearing every human grief on the Cross, of his victorious rising, living 'that death may die', but perhaps it's the verse that starts 'Crown Him the Lord of Peace' that seems particularly relevant in such a troubled world.

DEAR LORD AND FATHER OF MANKIND
John Greenleaf Whittier, 1807-1892

Dear Lord and Father of mankind,
    Forgive our foolish ways;
Reclothe us in our rightful mind;
In purer lives thy service find,
    In deeper reverence, praise.

In simple trust like theirs who heard
    Beside the Syrian sea
The gracious calling of the Lord,
Let us, like them, without a word
    Rise up and follow thee.

O sabbath rest by Galilee!
    O calm of hills above,
Where Jesus knelt to share with thee
The silence of eternity,
    Interpreted by love!

With that deep hush subduing all
    Our words and works that drown
The tender whisper of thy call,
As noiseless let thy blessing fall
    As fell thy manna down.

Drop thy still dews of quietness,
    Till all our strivings cease;
Take from our souls the strain and stress,
And let our ordered lives confess
    The beauty of thy peace.

Breathe through the heats of our desire
    Thy coolness and thy balm;
Let sense be dumb, let flesh retire;
Speak through the earthquake, wind, and fire,
    O still small voice of calm!

From time to time when preachers are in short supply or haven't turned up, church congregations indulge in a service of popular hymns. Very often it's the same old favourites that keep appearing on the list, but there is one which provokes a little chuckle from me as I sing it because I wonder if the person who has chosen it knows the strange background to the poem from which the hymn has been extracted. It is entitled 'The brewing of Soma' by John Greenleaf Whittier, and the last six verses are the ones that begin with these familiar words:

> 'Dear Lord and Father of mankind,
> Forgive our foolish ways.'

You may well wonder what 'Soma' has to do with the beautiful words of this hymn, and when you know you may wish that you had never found out! It was an Indian fungus which the Vedic priests would soak in milk, drink, pass through the bladder and then drink again. This somewhat unusual brewing process made a very intoxicating liquor indeed, and the priests used it in a religious ritual to induce hallucinations and ecstacies. Believe it or not, these are the 'foolish ways' to which Whittier refers in the first verse of the hymn.

The author, John Greenleaf Whittier, was an American Quaker. His ancestors had travelled with the Pilgrim Fathers, and like them, John was very critical of the ceremonies and music that were found in the churches around him. In his poem he describes these strange Indian rites and religious escapism and compares them to the sensuality he sees in Christian worship. Incense, decoration, sound; all these, he says, distract the mind, not focus it. One of the earlier verses reads:

> 'From tent to tent
> The Soma's sacred madness went,
> A storm of drunken joy.'

But then come these last six verses where Whittier puts forward his alternative. Think of some of the phrases he uses: 'Drop thy still dews of quietness'; 'Let sense be dumb, let flesh retire'; 'O still small voice of calm'.

Outside the meeting house, life was anything but calm. He was the editor of a Boston newspaper, and secretary of the American Anti-Slavery Society in 1836. He was often set upon by mobs of anti-abolitionists. Yet throughout this period of his life he continued to write such fine works that in his later years he was known as the 'Grand old man of poetry'. The Republican party even claim him as one of their spiritual founders. His words were listened to in high places!

I'm not sure that he would have really approved of his poems being set to music and sung as hymns. Even the lovely tune Repton that partners the hymn would, in his view, fall into the 'Soma' category. He even said on one occasion: 'I know nothing of music and do not claim to have written one hymn.'

But I know that a lot of people are very glad that the editors of 'Congregational Hymns' chose to include it in their collection of 1884, and it now appears in all the major hymnbooks. I think that we had better keep the recipe for 'Soma' under our hats, don't you?

ETERNAL FATHER
William Whiting, 1825-1878

Eternal Father, strong to save,
Whose arm doth bind the restless wave,
Who bidd'st the mighty ocean deep
Its own appointed limits keep:
　O hear us when we cry to thee
　For those in peril on the sea.

O Saviour, whose almighty word
The winds and waves submissive heard,
Who walkedst on the foaming deep,
And calm amid its rage didst sleep:

O sacred Spirit, who didst brood
Upon the chaos dark and rude,
Who bad'st its angry tumult cease,
And gavest light and life and peace:

O Trinity of love and power,
Our brethren shield in danger's hour;
From rock and tempest, fire and foe,
Protect them wheresoe'er they go:
　And ever let there rise to thee
　Glad hymns of praise from land and sea.

They were a fussy lot, those compilers of 'Hymns Ancient and Modern'! It seems that very few hymns appeared in the same form as the authors' first submissions.

> 'O Thou who biddst the ocean deep
> Its own appointed limits keep.'

Familiar words, but what are the opening lines?

Well, when William Whiting wrote them they *were* the opening lines, and 'Eternal Father, strong to save,' was in fact the fourth line. Perhaps if the hymn had remained in its original form it may never have become so popular. We shall never know.

It's strange that a hymn so full of strong images of the sea was written by a Winchester choirmaster who, as far as I know, had never set foot on a ship. There is a story that Whiting wrote it for one of his choristers who was about to set sail for America which could be true, but it's far more likely to have been inspired by parts of Milton's 'Paradise Lost.'

Whiting had always thought of himself as a poet, so it must have been disappointing when sales of his first collection of poems, 'Rural thoughts and scenes' published in 1850, were very few.

He had rather more success with his choristers. At first when he'd taken on the job at the age of seventeen, the boys were nothing more than 'fags' for the Scholars of Winchester College, but he soon licked them into musical shape and earned himself the reputation of a hard taskmaster. Perhaps he felt he had to compensate for his disability, a club foot, but the boys still called him 'Hoppy' behind his back.

Whiting stayed in the job for thirty-six years, living in a small lodge with his wife and three children, his mother and mother-in-law, the organist's apprentice, sixteen choristers, and old Auntie Amy and all. Perhaps on more than the odd occasion he longed to be out on the open sea!

'Eternal Father' has certainly been heard many times at sea and is, of course, brought out every year for Sea Sunday. It's universally acknowledged as the sailor's hymn, although I think there could be some competition these days from Rod Stewart's 'I am sailing'. The North Atlantic was the scene of perhaps the most famous of all its renditions, as Churchill and Roosevelt met on board HMS Prince of Wales during the Second World War. It was thought to be the most appropriate hymn to be sung at Divisions, and it does possess that air of dignity that lends itself to the special occasion.

I am absolutely certain that it would not have ever been considered in the version that you may have come across in a children's hymnbook,

> 'O hear us when we cry to you,
> For those who sail the ocean blue.'

It sounds more like a playground skipping rhyme! I'll stick to the original, well, almost the original.

FOR ALL THE SAINTS
William Walsham How, 1823-1897

For all the saints who from their labours rest,
Who thee by faith before the world confessed,
Thy name, O Jesus, be for ever blest:
    Alleluia, alleluia!

Thou wast their rock, their fortress, and their might;
Thou, Lord, their captain in the well-fought fight;
Thou in the darkness still their one true light:
    Alleluia, alleluia!

O may thy soldiers, faithful, true, and bold,
Fight as the saints who nobly fought of old,
And win, with them, the victor's crown of gold!
    Alleluia, alleluia!

O blest communion, fellowship divine!
We feebly struggle, they in glory shine;
Yet all are one in thee, for all are thine:
    Alleluia, alleluia!

And when the strife is fierce, the warfare long,
Steals on the ear the distant triumph song,
And hearts are brave again, and arms are strong:
    Alleluia, alleluia!

The golden evening brightens in the west;
Soon, soon to faithful warriors comes their rest;
Sweet is the calm of paradise the blest:
    Alleluia, alleluia!

But lo, there breaks a yet more glorious day:
The saints triumphant rise in bright array;
The King of Glory passes on his way!
    Alleluia, alleluia!

From earth's wide bounds, from ocean's farthest coast,
Through gates of pearl streams in the countless host,
Singing to Father, Son, and Holy Ghost:
    Alleluia, alleluia!

Fishing, fernery and frolicking around the dance floor were the abiding passions of William Walsham How, the author of the hymn 'For all the saints'. His Rectory garden in Whittington, Shrewsbury, had no less than five streams, and was ideal for growing the many different varieties of fern that the Victorians admired so much.

William How had taken up this position in 1851 when he was twenty-eight, and although he loved the grounds he didn't think much of the design of the church which had been built by a Mr Harrison during the incumbency of a Mr Davies, and so not long after the family was installed How wrote the following verse:

> 'We will not censure Mr Davies
> Now good man, he in his grave is,
> Nevertheless the Church you gave us,
> Ugly is beyond comparison
> O you dreadful Mr Harrison.'

A far cry from the verses of his great processional hymn!

Despite this one drawback, the Hows found Whittington very much to their taste and stayed there for twenty-eight years. William wrote many of his hymns during this period as well as being one of the three editors working with Sir Arthur Sullivan on the 1871 SPCK hymnbook. He may have liked his country sports and he certainly made sure he had his holidays, but during the rest of the year he worked very hard, and both he and his wife won the respect of the parish and beyond.

I suspect that he would have been quite happy to have seen out his days in Whittington but his fame had spread and when Mr Disraeli asked him to oversee the slums of London's East End as its Bishop he felt he must accept. Perhaps he did pine for his lovely garden. He could only manage a small greenhouse in the city, but he soon got involved with the grass roots of his church, and apparently could often be seen wearing a shovel hat, apron and gaiters with his clerical robes stuffed into an old bag which also housed a broken pastoral staff.

The children thought the world of him and he was nicknamed 'The Children's Bishop', and sometimes the 'Omnibus Bishop', because he loved using public transport. He would arrive at some churches clutching a small dais, because he was so short he couldn't be seen in some pulpits! The only blot on the landscape was his boss, the Bishop of London. They didn't see eye to eye on a few matters and eventually William, now a widower, was moved on to Wakefield.

Retirement was a state that William Walsham How chose to ignore. He was still working at the age of seventy-four, but died suddenly while on a fishing holiday in Ireland.

'For all the saints', based on the Te Deum, continues to be one of our most popular and uplifting hymns. You try singing those wonderful Alleluias sitting down!

GUIDE ME, O THOU GREAT JEHOVAH
William Williams, 1717-1791

Guide me, O thou great Jehovah,
    Pilgrim through this barren land;
I am weak, but thou art mighty;
    Hold me with thy powerful hand:
        Bread of heaven,
    Feed me now and evermore.

Open thou the crystal fountain,
    Whence the healing stream shall flow;
Let the fiery, cloudy pillar
    Lead me all my journey through:
        Strong Deliverer,
    Be thou still my strength and shield.

When I tread the verge of Jordan,
    Bid my anxious fears subside;
Death of death, and hell's destruction,
    Land me safe on Canaan's side:
        Songs of praises
    I will ever give to thee.

Amateur dramatics has been the great passion of my life for as long as I can remember but one of the most enjoyable and challenging plays that I have been involved with was a production of 'Under Milk Wood' by Dylan Thomas. I had to play three characters, all of whom had a slightly different Welsh accent and it took hours of practice to get the voices right. On the many occasions that I and other members of the company felt that we had bitten off rather more than we could chew, we would raise our spirits with a rousing chorus of 'Guide me, O Thou great Jehovah'. It always did the trick and I understand now why Welsh Rugby supporters sing it at the top of their voices to raise the morale of their team.

The tune Cwm Rhondda transports the listener to the mountains and valleys of Wales and if we're to follow in the footsteps of the hymnwriter we will need a stout pair of walking boots, or a good horse!

As a young medical student in 1738 William Williams happened to be passing Talgarth churchyard when he was stopped in his tracks by the thundering voice of Howell Harris, an itinerant preacher. The message was so powerful that it changed the course of William's life. He gave up medicine and became a preacher himself and although the Church wouldn't allow him to become a priest he was able to take up the post of deacon in the Episcopal church at Llanwrtyd.

Even there it wasn't easy, and he got into trouble for not making the sign of the cross at baptisms. He eventually resigned and joined the Calvinistic Methodists.

He took to the outdoor life, following the example of John Wesley and clocking up (or should that be clopping up!) almost one hundred thousand miles during the period known as the Methodist Revival.

William Williams wrote eight hundred hymns, all in his native language, but fortunately for the English speakers another Mr Williams in 1771 made the first translation of this hymn which has come to embody the spirit of the Welsh.

It was published at first in a leaflet form and later appeared in a book with the lengthy title of 'Collection of hymns sung in the Countess of Huntingdon's Chapels in Sussex'. In some hymn books 'Guide me, O thou great Redeemer' is the first line, a change of the editors of 'Hymns Ancient and Modern'. 'Jehovah' was obviously a title thought to be inappropriate by Anglicans in 1868!

I was surprised to find that the tune Cwm Rhondda wasn't written especially for the hymn but for a kind of Baptist Eisteddfod in 1905. It first appeared alongside the hymn in the 1933 Methodist hymnbook. There's a legendary story that the composer John Hughes, an official of the Great Western Railway, wrote it in chalk on a piece of tarpaulin, but his wife always insisted instead that he wrote it one Sunday morning while sitting in chapel. Obviously not a particularly riveting preacher that morning, unlike Howel Harris over a century and a half before.

The title that William Williams gave the hymn in 1745 was 'Nerth i fyned trwy'r Anialwch'. See if you can get your tongue round that!

HARK THE GLAD SOUND!
Philip Doddridge, 1702-1751

Hark the glad sound! The Saviour comes,
   The Saviour promised long;
Let every heart prepare a throne,
   And every voice a song.

He comes the prisoners to release,
   In Satan's bondage held;
The gates of brass before him burst,
   The iron fetters yield.

He comes the broken heart to bind,
   The bleeding soul to cure,
And with the treasures of his grace
   To enrich the humble poor.

Our glad hosannas, Prince of Peace,
   Thy welcome shall proclaim;
And heaven's eternal arches ring
   With thy belovèd name.

Where did they all sleep and how many sittings were needed to feed and water them? These are questions that I am continually asking myself as I look into the family life of the eighteenth century hymnwriters. We know Charles Wesley was child number eighteen out of nineteen, but the author of 'Hark the glad sound!' tops even that.

When baby Philip was welcomed into the Doddridge family in 1702 it was the twentieth time his mother had presented her husband with a bundle of joy. And, perhaps thankfully, it was to be the last. Imagine nineteen brothers and sisters to look up to. Would you ever remember all their names?

Although young Philip often suffered from ill health he did extraordinarily well at his school in St Albans and was noticed by the Duchess of Bedford, who offered to pay his University fees if he studied for holy orders. It was a wonderful opportunity indeed but Master Doddridge declined. His clergyman grandfather had been cruelly ejected from his living after the Act of Uniformity and Philip too carried the torch of dissent. No university would have accepted him, so like Isaac Watts he graduated from one of the Dissenting Academies, and six years later took charge of Castle Hill Chapel in Northampton.

Full of energy he launched himself into the local community, founded his own academy where John Wesley gave the occasional lecture, wrote 'The rise and progress of religion in the soul', which had a great influence on the Evangelical movement, co-founded a hospital and somehow, amid all this activity, found time to write four hundred hymns.

'Hark the glad sound!' was written to highlight the main points of Doddridge's Advent sermon in 1735. He often did this in the hopes that the message would stay in the minds of his congregation that little bit longer! Sadly the hymn itself proved somewhat long and at least three of the verses are missing from our modern hymnbooks.

> 'He comes from the thick films of vice
> To clear the mental ray
> And on the eyeballs of the blind
> To pour celestial day.'

I think you can see why that particular verse was edited out, but the other two seem harmless enough.

There is a story that the hymn was sung aboard the flagship of the American Fleet in 1854 as they landed off the coast of Japan. What the inhabitants made of it I don't know. Perhaps they thought it was some kind of war cry! However, many people do welcome the opportunity to sing this hymn during the season of Advent when we turn our thoughts to the coming of the Christ-child, and if you want to look up the actual text Philip Doddridge used on that Advent Sunday two hundred and fifty-eight years ago, it's Luke 4:18-19. I would love to have heard the sermon!

HOLY, HOLY, HOLY
Reginald Heber, 1783-1826

Holy, holy, holy, Lord God Almighty!
    Early in the morning our song shall rise to thee:
Holy, holy, holy, merciful and mighty,
    God in three Persons, blessèd Trinity!

Holy, holy, holy! All the saints adore thee,
    Casting down their golden crowns around the glassy sea;
Cherubim and seraphim falling down before thee,
    Who wert, and art, and evermore shalt be.

Holy, holy, holy! Though the darkness hide thee,
    Though the eye of sinful man thy glory may not see,
Only thou art holy; there is none beside thee,
    Perfect in power, in love, and purity.

Holy, holy, holy, Lord God Almighty!
    All thy works shall praise thy name in earth and sky and sea;
Holy, holy, holy, merciful and mighty,
    God in Three Persons, blessèd Trinity!

'Fat as a little mole' was one description of baby Reginald Heber as he took his first gasps of Cheshire air in 1783. His father was one of the Rectors of Malpas; there happened to be two Rectors for the same church due to an argument which had occurred seven hundred years previously.

It was in the 'Higher Rectory' that young Reginald was raised, along with his brother Thomas, sister May and half brother Dick who, in spite of being much older, became his preferred companion. In the countryside around their home Reginald and his brothers and sister caught eels, hunted and trapped. Then at the age of thirteen, Reginald Heber was sent to boarding school.

At first his parents couldn't understand why the money they gave him seemed to disappear so quickly, until it was revealed that he was giving it away to anyone who seemed to need it more than he did. The remedy was to sew the notes into his pocket linings before his journey to keep them intact, at least until he reached the school.

This concern for the welfare of those less fortunate was to be the hallmark of his life, because although he went on to a brilliant career at Oxford, winning prizes for English and Latin verse with friends like Walter Scott, he always found time for the ordinary parishioner, counselling and comforting, and as one of them describes, 'kneeling at sick beds at the hazard of his own life'.

There are really only two and a half of Heber's hymns that are well known today. One is the Epiphany hymn 'Brightest and best of the sons of the morning'. The 'half' is the first verse of the hymn we sing to the Welsh tune associated with the song 'All through the night'. Someone else finished it off! The other one, his most famous hymn, is 'Holy, Holy, Holy, Lord God Almighty'.

The strange thing is that Reginald Heber wasn't really very keen on hymns being sung in church. He was ordained in 1807 and with his wife Emily was appointed to the church at Moreton Say in Shropshire where he was plagued by Nonconformists. In his diary he notes, 'The Methodists here, are, thank God, not very numerous and I hope to diminish them still more.'

The singing of hymns, of course, was associated with these 'troublemakers' and so quite a few years passed before Rector Heber felt able to include hymns in his services.

It seemed to be a case of 'If you can't beat them, join them' because even he with his High Church background could see the advantages of using the hymn as a teaching tool, so he wrote a hymn for each Sunday and Feast Solemn Day. If you want to see Reginald's original scribbles, you'll have to look in his daughter's school sum book. 'Holy, Holy, Holy', the perfect paraphrase of Revelation 4 is written alongside the 'adds' and the 'takeaways'!

Reginald Heber's final years were spent in India as Bishop of Calcutta where the weather and workload took their toll, and he died at the age of forty-three. The Poet Laureate, Southey wrote the verse on his tombstone but I prefer R. H. Barham's rhyme which goes:

> 'A poet of no mean calibre
> I once knew and loved – dear Reginald Heber.'

HOW GREAT THOU ART
Carl Boberg, 1859-1940

O Lord my God! When I in awesome wonder
    Consider all the works thy hand hath made,
I see the stars, I hear the mighty thunder,
    Thy pow'r throughout the universe displayed:

> *Then sings my soul, my Saviour God, to thee,*
> *How great thou art! How great thou art!*
> *Then sings my soul, my Saviour God, to thee,*
> *How great thou art! How great thou art!*

When through the woods and forest glades I wander
    And hear the birds sing sweetly in the trees:
When I look down from lofty mountain grandeur,
    And hear the brook, and feel the gentle breeze:

And when I think: that God his Son not sparing,
    Sent him to die – I scarce can take it in:
That on the Cross, my burden gladly bearing,
    He bled and died, to take away my sin:

When Christ shall come with shout of acclamation
    And take me home – what joy shall fill my heart!
Then shall I bow in humble adoration,
    And there proclaim, my God how great thou art!

Copyright © 1953 Stuart K Hine/Thankyou Music, PO Box 75, Eastbourne, East Sussex BN23 6NW, UK. Worldwide (excl North America and Canada). Used by permission.

I first heard 'How Great thou Art' at a Billy Graham Crusade, many years ago now, but I remember that great soloist, George Beverley Shea, singing the verses, and then the choir joining him in the chorus:

> 'Then sings my soul, my Saviour God, to thee,
> How great thou art! How great thou art!'

By the third chorus I couldn't help but join in myself, and as the voices of thousands echoed around the stadium, I felt that these were words I wanted to sing again and again. I had no idea then what a fascinating story lay behind this hymn, of its many journeys and translations.

It begins on the South East coast of Sweden with a man named Carl Boberg, the son of a shipyard carpenter. In 1878, after hearing a sermon on sin and grace, he was convinced that he was a sinner and it was only when he heard a child trying to learn a verse from John's gospel that he accepted God's forgiveness. He went to Bible College for two years and then returned home to take up preaching at the tender age of twenty-one. It appears that one warm summer day, Carl and some friends were on their way home from evangelising the ladies of a local sewing class when they ran into a terrific storm. After sheltering for an hour, they witnessed the most perfect of rainbows, and on arrival at his house Carl immediately threw open the shutters to take another look. The view across the inlet, now so calm, combined with the song of the thrush, and the tolling of the church bell inspired him to write, and these are the original words:

> 'Then doth my soul burst forth in song of praise.
> O great God, O great God.'

The nine verses of the poem were published in a couple of periodicals, and as it wasn't written as a hymn, the author was very surprised when preaching in one of the provinces to hear his work being sung to an old Swedish melody. He liked it and in 1894 it appeared in the hymnbook of the Swedish Missionary Alliance, and thirteen years later in a German hymnbook, where 'O great God' had been translated, 'How great thou art.'

Later it appeared in a Russian book, and it was there that the man who translated it into English, Stuart Hine, first saw it, but at that time had no idea that its origins were Swedish. He actually changed it a good deal, his inspiration coming from the Russian mountain villages, as he wandered through the 'woods and forest glades', hearing the 'mighty thunder', and the birds singing 'sweetly in the trees'.

He published his version alongside the Russian version in 1949 and copies were sent to refugees from the war living in fifteen different countries. Wherever it was sung people loved it, and the hymn grew in popularity all over the world. It was taken to New Zealand where one rendition on the radio gave rise to an enormous response from the public.

It is still a great favourite today, and not before time, it has started to appear in some of the newer mainstream hymnbooks.

IN CHRIST THERE IS NO EAST OR WEST
John Oxenham, 1852-1941

In Christ there is no east or west,
   In him no south or north,
But one great fellowship of love
   Throughout the whole wide earth.

In him shall true hearts everywhere
   Their high communion find,
His service is the golden cord
   Close-binding all mankind.

Join hands, then, brothers of the faith,
   Whate'er your race may be;
Who serves my Father as a son
   Is surely kin to me.

In Christ now meet both east and west,
   In him meet south and north,
All Christlike souls are one in him,
   Throughout the whole wide earth.

As the organist played over the first line of the hymn, I automatically looked down at the end of it to see who the author was. The name John Oxenham rang a distant bell as I began to sing 'In Christ there is no East or West', but it was some weeks afterwards that I remembered where I'd seen the name before.

As a child I'd won a prize for Bible reading in a local inter-church Speech and Drama Festival, a novel entitled 'The Hidden Years' which centred around the boyhood of Jesus. It was one of my favourite stories, and I read it over and over again. John Oxenham was the author and these memories made me look again at the hymn.

The first thing I learned was that his real name was William Arthur Dunkerley, born in Cheetham in 1852, but he wrote under a *nom de plume* because he was painfully shy. Even some of his closest friends didn't know about his 'other life'. They just saw him as a deacon and a Bible class leader in the Congregational Church and he was able to keep his writing secret for many years.

Readers of Kingsley's 'Westwood Ho!' will know that John Oxenham is the name of the expedition leader so this may have been one of our author's favourite books.

William Dunkerley was a businessman and regularly travelled abroad. On one of his trips he met Jerome K. Jerome of 'Three men in a boat' fame, and he took yet another name, Julian Ross, in order to go into partnership with Jerome in a publishing venture. Eventually his writing became so successful that he gave up his job in business and concentrated on what he enjoyed doing most.

The hymn 'In Christ there is no East or West' was originally part of a libretto for a pageant called 'Darkness and Light' which was produced in 1908 in the Agricultural Hall for the London Missionary Society. Quite a few hymns seem to have started life at one of the many LMS meetings! Then it was included in the 'Bees in Amber' collection, but it first appeared as a hymn in the 'Songs of Praise' book and is still in many of our new ones.

The tune that is often coupled with it, McKee, has an interesting history. It is from a Negro Spiritual song, 'I know the angels done changed my name', which was adapted in 1939 by a chorister at St George's Church in New York, who named it after the rector, Elmer McKee. I've often wondered why!

William Dunkerley, alias Julian Ross, alias John Oxenham died in Worthing in 1941, and just before he died, he lost consciousness and had a vision of the life to come which was so vivid that his daughter wrote it down and it was published under the title 'Out of the body'. Perhaps it was one of those experiences which so many people describe as being brought 'back from the brink'.

'In Christ there is no East or West' is a favourite hymn during One World Week and as the theme is one of the universality of Christ and the fellowship within the world wide Church, it seems to me to be a hymn that is both a comfort and a challenge, and worth including regularly in our services.

IN THE BLEAK MID-WINTER
Christina Georgina Rossetti, 1830-1894

In the bleak mid-winter
    Frosty wind made moan,
Earth stood hard as iron,
    Water like a stone;
Snow had fallen, snow on snow,
    Snow on snow,
In the bleak mid-winter,
    Long ago.

Our God, heav'n cannot hold him,
    Nor earth sustain;
Heav'n and earth shall flee away
    When he comes to reign.
In the bleak mid-winter
    A stable-place sufficed
The Lord God Almighty,
    Jesus Christ.

Angels and archangels
    May have gathered there,
Cherubim and seraphim
    Throngèd the air –
But his mother only,
    In her maiden bliss,
Worshipped the Belovèd
    With a kiss.

What can I give him,
    Poor as I am?
If I were a shepherd
    I would bring a lamb;
If I were a wise man
    I would do my part;
Yet what I can I give him –
    Give my heart.

Dante Gabriel and William Michael Rossetti, along with their younger sister Christina Georgina, seemed to possess all the talents that Victorian society admired so much.

Their father was an Italian who, disillusioned by politics, left his native land as a young man to seek a freer environment. He was made Professor of Italian at King's College, London, and married a lively and intelligent wife, Frances, who bore three children and, like so many women of her era, was responsible for the education of her daughter.

Christina was a beautiful and intelligent girl with dark eyes and black hair. She was so striking that Holman Hunt used her as a model for the face of Christ in one of his paintings. At the age of twelve she had her first book of poems published and although it was her brother Dante, as the leader of a group of poets and artists known as the 'Pre-Raphaelite Brotherhood', who achieved most acclaim, the rather delicate home-loving Christina was also making a name for herself with a best selling anthology entitled 'Goblin Market'.

Such beauty and talent were bound to attract a number of suitors and the first to make overtures was a young painter, James Collinson. Christina was captivated. The only problem was that he was a Catholic and she a devout Anglican. In the first flush of love he vowed to embrace her faith but on reflection felt unable to take such a drastic step, and so the engagement was broken.

Her next suitor was W. B. Scott, and another relationship blossomed until it was revealed that he was not the man she took him for. He was married, and also had a number of mistresses. It was a terrible shock for the Rossetti family and yet Christina couldn't bear a separation. She met Mrs Scott, and although the three of them became firm friends, her misfortune in love left deep emotional scars. Many of her poems written around this time are on the subject of unrequited love. As the years went by she turned more and more to her faith, and when she was given a last chance to marry another admirer she politely refused and became pre-occupied with poems commending divine love rather than human passion.

'Love came down at Christmas', is one of her poems that has become a great favourite, but 'In the bleak mid-winter' is even more popular. Christina sets the scene for the Incarnation in a typical British winter, with the whole of Bethlehem covered in a blanket of white snow, and yet it is in no way sentimental. We're reminded of the contrast between the first coming and the second coming of Christ and the final verse asks for a response from the reader or singer:

'What can I give him, poor as I am?'

Christina Georgina Rossetti died just a few days after Christmas 1894 at the age of sixty-four. In her last years she seemed to be a rather melancholy character, sometimes compared to Tennyson's 'Lady of Shalott', and yet as a friend commented after her death, "Her faith and love were the motive powers of her life. She never obtruded her piety, yet I felt I was in the presence of a holy woman."

Perhaps Holman Hunt's canvas was not the only place on which to see the face of Christ.

IT CAME UPON THE MIDNIGHT CLEAR
Edmund Hamilton Sears, 1810-1876

It came upon the midnight clear,
    That glorious song of old,
From angels bending near the earth
    To touch their harps of gold:
Peace on the earth, good-will to men,
    From heaven's all gracious King!
The world in solemn stillness lay
    To hear the angels sing.

Still through the cloven skies they come
    With peaceful wings unfurled;
And still their heavenly music floats
    O'er all the weary world;
Above its sad and lowly plains
    They bend on hovering wing,
And ever o'er its Babel sounds
    The blessèd angels sing.

But with the woes of sin and strife
    The world has suffered long;
Beneath the angel strain have rolled
    Two thousand years of wrong;
And man, at war with man, hears not
    The love song which they bring:
O hush the noise, ye men of strife,
    And hear the angels sing.

And ye, beneath life's crushing load,
    Whose forms are bending low,
Who toil along the climbing way
    With painful steps and slow –
Look now! for glad and golden hours
    Come swiftly on the wing:
O rest beside the weary road,
    And hear the angels sing.

For lo! the days are hastening on,
    By prophet bards foretold,
When with the ever-circling years
    Comes round the age of gold.
When peace shall over all the earth
    Its ancient splendours fling,
And the whole world give back the song
    Which now the angels sing.

When is a carol not a carol? When it's an 'Ethical Song' of course! It seems that one of our best-loved Christmas hymns was never intended to be sung exclusively around the festive season. It is true that the verses of 'It came upon the midnight clear' are inspired by the message of the angels to the shepherds but its theme is world peace, not an account of the Nativity. 'Protest song' would be a better genre under which to file it and the social message it contains becomes even clearer when the historical background to the hymn is revealed.

The author of the 'carol', Edmund Hamilton Sears, was born in 1810, in Sandisfield, Massachusetts. He was a Unitarian minister, which is strange, considering that he often preached on the divinity of Christ and even wrote a book about it.

But it's the title of one of his other publications, 'Foregleams of Immortality', that caught my eye. I wonder if you can still get hold of it? Fascinating reading, I'm sure! He wrote only two hymns. 'Calm on the listening ear of night comes heaven's strains' really was intended for Christmas. 'It came upon the midnight clear' was first published in 1849 in a book called 'Christian Register', and it was around this time that tension was building between the forces of North and South which finally erupted in the Civil War. New England was also going through the birth pains of the Industrial Revolution and it was the era when the forty-niners all rushed to California hoping to find gold and make their fortune. The whole area was in a state of upheaval and this song addresses all these social concerns.

Edmund Sears calls it a 'Babel' and in the fourth verse, he describes the plight of so many of the people to whom he ministered.

> 'And ye beneath life's crushing load,
>   Whose forms are bending low,
> Who toil along the climbing way,
>   With painful steps and slow'.

It's a very long carol but I feel sorry that that particular verse and the following one have been omitted in some of the modern hymn and carol books because it seems to me to reflect just the kind of pressure and weariness that so many people can identify with in a world that is still in the midst of upheaval.

The last verse is an optimistic one where Edmund Sears asks his singers to look forward to and to work for a new Golden Age, not based on greed and materialism but one:

> 'When peace shall over all the world
>   Its ancient splendours fling,
> And the whole world gives back the song
>   Which now the angels sing'.

Isn't this a hymn that needs to be sung all the year round and not just to be brought out at Christmas?

IT IS GOD WHO HOLDS THE NATIONS
Fred Pratt Green, 1903-

It is God who holds the nations in the hollow of his hand;
It is God whose light is shining in the darkness of the land;
It is God who builds his City on the Rock and not on sand:
    May the living God be praised!

It is God whose purpose summons us to use the present hour;
Who recalls us to our senses when a nation's life turns sour;
In the discipline of freedom we shall know his saving power:
    May the living God be praised!

When a thankful nation, looking back, has cause to celebrate
Those who win our admiration by their service to the state;
When self-giving is a measure of the greatness of the great:
    May the living God be praised!

He reminds us every sunrise that the world is ours on lease:
For the sake of life tomorrow may our love for it increase;
May all races live together, share its riches, be at peace:
    May the living God be praised!

Reproduced by permission of Stainer & Bell Ltd.

Fred Pratt Green, the author of 'It is God who holds the nations in the hollow of his hand' may not have such an impressive sounding name as Augustus Toplady or Sabine Baring-Gould, but if you take time to read his poetry and study his hymns, you will find a very special person behind the name.

Some years ago, in my quest for anecdotes, I wrote to Fred, and in return received a lively and humorous letter, full of fascinating information and personal reflection.

He told me that his father had intended to emigrate to America, but on reaching Liverpool, he met a distant relative and decided to stay, making a new life for himself manufacturing leather goods. Fred was born in 1903, on the borders of Broad Green and Roby, and although his father was a Wesleyan, his mother was an Anglican, and on Sunday mornings they would walk across the fields to Childwall Parish Church. On their removal to Wallasey in 1912 they found that the Wesleyan Chapel was just around the corner and so they all became members there.

The change must have suited Fred as he later became a Methodist minister, first appointed to a church in Yorkshire and then, on the day war broke out in 1939, moving down to the London area. It was during this period that he began to write, inspired by the father of a boy from an Enfield Sunday School, who, although crippled by arthritis, had a great interest in poetry. They met regularly to criticise each other's work and eventually, after gaining what Fred describes as a 'modest' reputation, he was contacted in 1963 by the Committee in charge of producing the Supplement to the Methodist Hymn Book and invited to submit some modern hymns.

Most of the Pratt Green hymns seem to fall into two categories. First, he enjoyed entering hymnwriting competitions. 'What shall our greeting be?' was the winner of an event organised by Queen's Ecumenical College in Birmingham to find a new hymn on Christian unity.

Then there were the requests. There were scores of them, such as the one written for a Presbyterian Church in a suburb of Chicago. They wanted a hymn for their 150th anniversary which would contain a reference to the Gospel Riders who were active in spreading the gospel in the Mid-West. Fred had decided on a line which included the phrase 'With Bibles in their saddlebags', until he was told this would not do at all because in Arlington Heights, Chicago, 'saddlebags' was slang for women's thighs!

A stranger story surrounds the hymn 'It is God who holds the nations'. It was written at the request of the Dean of Norwich for use at the celebration of the Queen's Silver Jubilee in 1977. Alan Webster, Inter Dean of St Paul's, happened to pass on a copy before the event to the Dean of York Minster, who in turn happened to have it in his pocket when he went up to London to the committee appointed to draw up an Order of Service for use in all the Churches for the occasion. (The printing was held up because the hymn commissioned from John Betjeman, the Poet Laureate, was felt to be quite unsuitable.) The Dean of York produced a piece of paper from his pocket and it was a very surprised Fred who received a telephone call from Lambeth Palace asking permission to use his hymn!

Fred Pratt Green is certainly one of our most prolific modern hymnwriters, contributing to over one hundred hymnbooks. It comes as no surprise to hear that all his royalties go into a Trust Fund for the encouragement of Church Music, helping other writers to practise their craft and so join the noble line of men and women who have contributed to such an important part of our worship. Perhaps they too secretly hope that one day their hymn will be produced from a pocket at just the right moment!

LEAD US, HEAVENLY FATHER, LEAD US
James Edmeston, 1791-1867

Lead us, heavenly Father, lead us
   O'er the world's tempestuous sea;
Guard us, guide us, keep us, feed us,
   For we have no help but thee,
Yet possessing every blessing
   If our God our Father be.

Saviour, breathe forgiveness o'er us;
   All our weakness thou dost know;
Thou didst tread this earth before us,
   Thou didst feel its keenest woe;
Lone and dreary, faint and weary,
   Through the desert thou didst go.

Spirit of our God, descending,
   Fill our hearts with heavenly joy,
Love with every passion blending,
   Pleasure that can never cloy;
Thus provided, pardoned, guided,
   Nothing can our peace destroy.

James Edmeston was an architect, whose work sometimes took him to the London Orphan Asylum. Many of the children who lived there were illegitimate and had been abandoned as babies, left on rubbish dumps or outside Church gates. In the early 1800s no family wanted the shame or the scandal which an unmarried mother brought. James Edmeston was very impressed by the Christian work that was being done at what had originally been called the 'Foundling Hospital' and when his business was completed he would stay on, talking to the children, helping out with chores, supporting the cause in whatever ways he could.

James felt inspired to write nearly two thousand hymns especially for the children in the orphanage. Every Sunday morning he would set some time aside and come up with some verses which he then read at Family Worship.

Some biographical accounts describe him as a drab and rather grey character but a man who can dream up such hymnbook titles as 'The Cottage Minstrel' and 'Infant Breathings', surely had more than just a touch of colour in his life.

It seems a pity that out of so many hymns only one has survived into our modern collections, but 'Lead us, heavenly Father, lead us' is exceptionally popular, especially for marriage services. It was sung at the Princess Royal's wedding in 1922 and at the Queen Mother's the following year.

There's just one line in verse two that some people might take issue with: 'Lone and dreary, faint and weary, through the desert thou didst go.' It's that word 'dreary' that perhaps today has a slightly different connotation and I see that in 'Hymns for Today's Church' the line has been changed to 'Tempted, taunted, yet undaunted'. I must say I quite like that, although I don't know what the author would have thought about it. Who knows, maybe he just couldn't find another rhyme for 'weary' and time was pressing!

James Edmeston may not be a familiar name to most of us but one of his pupils in architecture, George Gilbert Scott, worked on the restoration of Cathedrals and designed some of the great London landmarks such as St Pancras Station and the Albert Memorial. Scott's grandson was the architect of the great Anglican Cathedral in Liverpool.

MINE EYES HAVE SEEN THE GLORY
Julia Ward Howe, 1819-1910

Mine eyes have seen the glory of the coming of the Lord;
He is trampling out the vintage where the grapes of wrath are stored;
He has loosed the fateful lightning of his terrible swift sword:
His truth is marching on.
    Glory, glory, alleluia!
    Glory, glory, alleluia!
    Glory, glory, alleluia!
His truth is marching on.

He has sounded forth the trumpet that shall never call retreat;
He is sifting out the hearts of men before his judgement-seat:
O be swift, my soul, to answer him; be jubilant, my feet!
Our God is marching on.
    Glory, glory, alleluia!
    Glory, glory, alleluia!
    Glory, glory, alleluia!
Our God is marching on.

In the beauty of the lilies Christ was born across the sea,
With a glory in his bosom that transfigures you and me;
As he died to make men holy, let us live to make men free,
While God is marching on.
    Glory, glory, alleluia!
    Glory, glory, alleluia!
    Glory, glory, alleluia!
While God is marching on.

Julia Ward Howe was a woman to be reckoned with. Feminism, penal reform and preaching in the Unitarian Church were just a few of the many causes and activities that featured in her busy life. It was also an extremely aristocratic life. Her father was a rich American banker, descended from one of Oliver Cromwell's officers who fled England and the Restoration of Charles II, and the family moved in the upper class circles of high society. They actually knew the original Jones's, the couple everyone aspired to 'keep up with'!

That was unimportant to the Ward family. They had enough airs and graces of their own; it's said of Julia's brother, Sam, that he was the only man in America who was capable of strutting when sitting down! Their mother was a patron of the arts who ensured that her daughter was given every opportunity to experience the finer things of life, particularly encouraging her interest in music and writing.

There must have been scores of young 'hopefuls' lining up with offers of marriage, but it was a rather older 'hopeful' who won the hand of the lovely Julia. Dr Howe from Boston was a well-known philanthropist nineteen years her senior, and his new wife adapted easily to her new life of crusades and causes that was to take her across America and even into Europe.

Yet it was none of these worthy campaigns that made Julia Ward Howe a household name. It was a man called John Brown. He was a more than slightly mad religious zealot who planned to become king over a community of liberated slaves in the mountains, but before his dream was fully realised, he was caught and hanged for murder and treason. The Northern soldiers during the Civil War looked upon him as a folk-hero, and often sang about his exploits, and it was one such song that Dr and Mrs Howe heard one night when visiting the Union troops.

'John Brown's body lies a-moulding in the grave, but his soul goes marching on.' She was very moved as she sat in her tent listening to the stirring sound of the soldiers' voices, and it was a friend who had accompanied Dr and Mrs Howe who suggested she should write some of her own words to the marching tune, and make it into a hymn. It was finished by the morning, and very soon acclaimed as the Battle Hymn of the Republic. Mrs Howe was showered with honours, and the popularity of her hymn grew.

'Glory, Glory, Hallelujah' arrived in Britain in 1896, appearing in Garret Horder's 'Treasury of Hymns', and today it still features in many modern hymnbooks. It's a definite favourite with marching bands, and although I have to admit to singing 'teacher hit me with a ruler', and 'rubbing the chest with camphor, camphor, camphorated oil', (in my youth of course) it's a hymn that shouts of God's ultimate victory. Julia Ward Howe's hymn and our God are still marching on.

NEARER, MY GOD, TO THEE
Sarah Flower Adams, 1805-1848

Nearer, my God, to thee,
   Nearer to thee!
E'en though it be a cross
   That raiseth me,
Still all my song shall be:
'Nearer, my God, to thee,
   Nearer to thee!'

Though, like the wanderer,
   The sun gone down,
Darkness be over me,
   My rest a stone,
Yet in my dreams I'd be
Nearer, my God, to thee,
   Nearer to thee!

There let the way appear
   Steps unto heaven –
All that thou sendest me
   In mercy given –
Angels to beckon me
Nearer, my God, to thee,
   Nearer to thee!

Then, with my waking thoughts
   Bright with thy praise,
Out of my stony griefs
   Bethel I'll raise;
So by my woes to be
Nearer, my God, to thee,
   Nearer to thee!

Or if on joyful wing
   Cleaving the sky,
Sun, moon, and stars forgot,
   Upwards I fly,
Still all my song shall be:
'Nearer, my God, to thee,
   Nearer to thee!'

The question everybody asks about the hymn 'Nearer my God to Thee' is, 'Was it or was it not sung as the 'Titanic' sank beneath the waves?' Is the story of the small band of musicians striking up the famous tune just folk-lore, or did those still on board really join in the singing of this popular hymn?

It is certainly a story one would love to be true. The idea that a Baptist minister could, with all the panic going on around him, ask the little string group to play this hymn of comfort and hope is something one would like to think possible. One of the few survivors, I believe still living, Eva Hart is convinced of its authenticity, and that hymns were being played has been verified by a number of people, but whether 'Nearer my God' was the last to be played is still open to question.

I don't know what the author of the hymn would have made of all this. I think she would have appreciated the drama of the situation, as Sarah Fuller Flower (yes, that really was her name!) had a brief career as an actress. In 1834 she married William Adams, when the Fuller was dropped, but the Flower was kept, and so we find the name Sarah Flower Adams at the bottom of her hymns.

Illness prevented her from treading the boards for very long but she found fame following in her father's footsteps. He was a Radical journalist and Sarah became part of the literary set. The poet Robert Browning was a particular friend, and it's said that she was the model for 'Pauline', his first published poem.

Sarah attended the Unitarian Church and thirteen of her hymns, including 'Nearer my God', were published in a book used by the congregation in Finsbury. Later, in 1853, it was added to the most widely used Unitarian hymnbook and eventually was included in 'Hymns Ancient and Modern' and many other major collections.

However, Sarah's hymns always attracted a lot of controversy. Some people questioned whether Unitarian hymns should be sung by Trinitarian congregations. There was no mention of Christ, and so some editors hurriedly composed an additional verse to make it more acceptable. In our modern hymnbooks we seem to have reverted back to Sarah's original work with apparently very few complaints.

If it's one of your favourite hymns you'll know that it's based on Jacob's dream at Bethel where he sees the ladder stretching from earth to heaven, with the angels ascending and descending. At a time when he feels so alone Jacob is reminded that the channels of communication are always open. And so in her hymn Sarah Flower Adams reminds us that no matter how far away from God we feel, his presence is always near.

O COME, O COME, IMMANUEL
(*translated by*) John Mason Neale, 1818-1866

O come, O come, Immanuel,
And ransom captive Israel,
That mourns in lonely exile here
Until the Son of God appear:
    Rejoice! Rejoice! Immanuel
    Shall come to thee, O Israel.

O come, O come, thou Lord of might,
Who to thy tribes, on Sinai's height,
In ancient times didst give the law
In cloud, and majesty, and awe:

O come, thou Rod of Jesse, free
Thine own from Satan's tyranny;
From depths of hell thy people save,
And give them vict'ry o'er the grave:

O come, thou Key of David, come,
And open wide our heav'nly home;
Make safe the way that leads on high,
And close the path to misery:

O come, thou Day-spring, come and cheer
Our spirits by thine advent here;
Disperse the gloomy clouds of night,
And death's dark shadows put to flight:

The history of the Advent hymn 'O Come, O Come, Immanuel', originally written in Latin, reaches back to at least the ninth century and comes from the monastic tradition. Each evening of the week before Christmas during the service of Vespers, some of the monks would lead the singing of an antiphon before and after the Magnificat. The precentor would sing one verse and then the congregation would reply with theirs. The seven antiphons used before Christmas were called the 'seven Os', as they all started with a long, drawn out O . . . h to symbolise the singers' great longing for Jesus, and their wonder at the mystery of the Incarnation.

Each antiphon emphasized a different aspect of Christ's character and used one of the Old Testament descriptions of the Messiah:

> O . . . Root of Jesse
> O . . . Dayspring
> O . . . Key of David

The last of them began 'O . . . Immanuel'. In the Latin the initials of the seven descriptions read backwards spell 'Ero Cras' which means 'Tomorrow I shall be there'. One wonders whether the congregations ever worked out the acrostic, or whether it was a secret known only to the hierarchy. It wasn't until the eighteenth century that someone in Germany had the idea of putting them all together into one hymn and the first version of it appeared in Cologne.

Much later in Britain, John Mason Neale made his own translation which started with the words 'Draw Nigh, Draw Nigh Immanuel'. He was quite a character. He achieved an ordinary degree from Cambridge but was hopeless at maths. However, he still managed to become a Fellow and took Holy Orders, but he was so 'High Church' that he fell out with his bishop and was suspended for fourteen years.

During this time, John Mason Neale founded an alms house, a school and an orphanage and in his spare time he dedicated himself to the promotion of what he called 'proper liturgical practice in the Church of England'! He studied all the ancient and medieval hymnology and became quite a notable authority on the subject, translating from the Latin so that congregations could enjoy the richness of those early hymns.

O GOD, OUR HELP IN AGES PAST
Isaac Watts, 1674-1748

O God, our help in ages past,
    Our hope for years to come,
Our shelter from the stormy blast,
    And our eternal home;

Under the shadow of thy throne
    Thy saints have dwelt secure;
Sufficient is thine arm alone,
    And our defence is sure.

Before the hills in order stood
    Or earth received her frame,
From everlasting thou art God,
    To endless years the same.

A thousand ages in thy sight
    Are like an evening gone,
Short as the watch that ends the night
    Before the rising sun.

The busy tribes of flesh and blood,
    With all their cares and fears,
Are carried downward by the flood,
    And lost in following years.

Time, like an ever-rolling stream,
    Bears all its sons away;
They fly forgotten, as a dream
    Dies at the opening day.

O God, our help in ages past,
    Our hope for years to come,
Be thou our guard while life shall last,
    And our eternal home.

'If you don't like the old book then I suggest you write something better!'

What a challenge for the little boy who in the 1680s found the metrical psalms so dull and repetitive. Within a week the young Isaac Watts had written his first hymn and presented it to his father, and it was sung the following Sunday at the Independent Chapel in Southampton where the family worshipped regularly.

Isaac Watts' first simple verses proved immensely popular as they were so different from what had gone before. People loved his freedom of expression and the later paraphrases of the Psalms where he 'makes David a Christian', were received and sung with great enthusiasm. Of course, many in the congregation could not read and so Isaac often had to teach them the verses one by one, or even line by line.

His boyhood was far from easy. His father refused to accept the Act of Uniformity and was twice thrown into prison, but his son stood by him, even though it meant sacrificing a university place at Oxford or Cambridge. Instead Isaac Watts enrolled at the Dissenting Academy in Stoke Newington, and after qualifying he became tutor to the son of an eminent Puritan. He was also in demand as a preacher and before long was asked to be pastor of one of the most exclusive congregations in London, Mark Lane Independent Chapel.

Dr Johnson was a contemporary of Watts and he disapproved of the new style of singing, although he was magnanimous enough to admit, 'It is sufficient for Watts to have done better than others what no man has done well'!

It's hard for us to imagine a time when there were no hymns, and to think that such favourites as 'When I survey the wondrous cross' and 'Joy to the world' stand at the very beginning of the history of hymnody. 'O God, our help in ages past' is a hymn from Watts' 'Psalms of David' collection and one which has become an integral part of any Remembrance Day Service. The version we sing today isn't quite the original. John Wesley made some changes to it in 1738, but it's still a hymn of enormous strength. The rhythm never falters and the words remind us of the permanence of God compared with the frailty of the human race.

Isaac Watts, despite his poor health, lived until he was seventy-five and in his latter years he was cared for by two of his devoted congregation. His death-bed scene is well documented, as they all were in those days. Every last detail was written down and Watts' final words taken down in shorthand, but the man himself had already laid plans. He wanted to be buried without any fuss in the Dissenting Chapel cemetery at Bunhill fields and he'd written his own epitaph. However, those left behind wanted more than that, and if you visit Westminster Abbey you will find his monument there.

Isaac Watts was not much to look at: he stood at just five feet, with a head that seemed to be much too large for his tiny body. But in hymnwriting terms he stands tall, richly deserving the title, 'Father of the British hymn'.

O JESUS, I HAVE PROMISED
John Ernest Bode, 1816-1874

O Jesus, I have promised
    To serve thee to the end;
Be thou for ever near me,
    My master and my friend;
I shall not fear the battle
    If thou art by my side,
Nor wander from the pathway
    If thou wilt be my guide.

O let me feel thee near me;
    The world is ever near;
I see the sights that dazzle,
    The tempting sounds I hear;
My foes are ever near me,
    Around me and within;
But, Jesus, draw thou nearer,
    And shield my soul from sin.

O let me hear thee speaking
    In accents clear and still,
Above the storms of passion,
    The murmurs of self-will;
O speak to reassure me,
    To hasten or control;
O speak, and make me listen,
    Thou guardian of my soul.

O Jesus, thou hast promised
    To all who follow thee,
That where thou art in glory
    There shall thy servant be;
And, Jesus, I have promised
    To serve thee to the end;
O give me grace to follow
    My master and my friend!

Whenever I ask people to name their favourite hymn most of them find it very difficult to choose just one, and even when we invited listeners to write in to Radio Merseyside as part of our search for the region's 'Top Ten', they still put forward at least two or three. Eventually we did come up with an overall winner, but I was very surprised to find that our Number One was neither a classic like 'The Lord's my Shepherd' nor a more modern hymn like 'Shine, Jesus Shine', but what I would call a good 'middle of the road' hymn, 'O Jesus, I have promised to serve Thee to the end'. Perhaps I should not have been surprised as on reflection this is a hymn that appeals to all age groups and has attracted a number of different tunes, old and new.

The words of the hymn were written in the middle of the nineteenth century by John Ernest Bode, a young man from the privileged classes of Victorian England. He attended Eton, Charterhouse and Christchurch, Oxford, where he was ordained a priest in the Church of England. He made his home in Oxford for a while but then moved his family to Cambridgeshire when he took the living in Castle Camps.

I'm not sure whether he read English at University but throughout his life John's love of poetry led him to write a considerable number of verses himself. His poetry was well regarded by all accounts, as he was nominated for the poetry professorship at Oxford in 1857. He lost by only one vote and it was Matthew Arnold who took up that coveted position.

So he turned his attention to hymns and wrote regularly for his own congregation. He particularly enjoyed writing for special occasions, such as Harvest, Christmas and Lent, and for the many baptisms and marriages at which he officiated.

But it was for an extra special day that he wrote the hymn, 'O Jesus, we have promised to serve thee to the end.' No, I haven't made a mistake, because the 'we' were his two sons and daughter and the occasion was their confirmation.

I know a little of what it's like to have a hymn written especially for you, as a friend once composed one to celebrate my recognition as a Methodist Local Preacher. It is something I treasure and I am sure that John Bode's children treasured the hymn that their father had written for them, as a prayer on their day of commitment.

The hymn is based on John 12:26: 'If any man serve me let him follow me, and where I am, there shall also my servant be.'

But whether it's a 'special day' or not, everyone can use this hymn to re-dedicate themselves in the service of God, and judging by its popularity it's something that we all feel the need to do quite often.

ONWARD, CHRISTIAN SOLDIERS
Sabine Baring-Gould, 1834-1924

Onward, Christian soldiers,
   Marching as to war,
With the cross of Jesus
   Going on before!
Christ, the royal master,
   Leads against the foe;
Forward into battle,
   See! His banners go!
*   Onward, Christian soldiers,*
*   Marching as to war,*
*   With the cross of Jesus*
*   Going on before!*

At the sign of triumph
   Satan's host doth flee;
On then, Christian soldiers,
   On to victory!
Hell's foundations quiver
   At the shout of praise;
Brothers, lift your voices;
   Loud your anthems raise:

Crowns and thrones may perish,
   Kingdoms rise and wane,
But the church of Jesus
   Constant will remain;
Gates of hell can never
   'Gainst that church prevail;
We have Christ's own promise,
   And that cannot fail:

Onward, then, ye people!
   Join our happy throng;
Blend with ours your voices
   In the triumph-song:
Glory, laud, and honour
   Unto Christ the King!
This through countless ages
   Men and angels sing:

Sabine Baring-Gould. A name not easily forgotten, and one which certainly reflects the colourful and somewhat exotic background of the author of the hymn 'Onward, Christian Soldiers'.

He was the grandson of an Admiral and son of an Indian Cavalryman, who was educated at home, but he often accompanied his parents as they visited the fashionable cities of Europe in the 1840s. Despite this unusual upbringing he managed to get into Clare College, Cambridge, and afterwards taught for a while. He was then ordained into the Church of England, married a beautiful mill-girl half his age, and in 1872 inherited his father's land in Devon and became the Squire-Parson and lord of all he surveyed.

Yet Sabine was not one to sit back. How can you when you have fourteen children? Maybe they were the reason for shutting himself in his room and writing so many books. He collected West Country Folk Songs, wrote 'The Lives of the Saints' in sixteen volumes, various travel books, novels and biographies – one hundred and fifty-nine publications in all, and yet what do we remember him for? The words of one popular hymn.

It's a hymn often associated with the Salvation Army, because of its image of the Christian Soldier taken from 2 Timothy, but its origin is not in Booth's East End of London, but in Horbury Bridge, Yorkshire. Reverend Baring-Gould was curate there in 1865 and it was customary in those parts on Whit Monday for all the children to march around the parish holding banners aloft, finishing the day in a marquee enjoying the tea and buns. Many of us living in North-West England still take part in a similar event on our Walking Days.

Reverend Baring-Gould wanted a nice orderly procession, and felt a good marching hymn would keep the children in line, and so, not happy with any of the words in the existing hymnbook, he took a suitable tune, St Albans, or Haydn as it is sometimes known, and wrote his own. He didn't start it until the evening before the march, but by the time the Sunday School scholars assembled the next day it was ready, and 'Onward Christian Soldiers' was sung for the first time.

Today some people criticise its use, believing its militaristic images are inappropriate, but I find it ironic that its very first criticism concerned the lines:

> 'We are not divided
> All one body we,'

This apparently gave offence and when it appeared in 'Hymns Ancient and Modern' the lines had been altered to:

> 'Though divisions harass,
> All one body we,'

Interestingly, 'Hymns and Psalms' omits the whole verse!

The tune that we are familiar with is not the original, but one written by Sir Arthur Sullivan especially for the hymn. It's a tune that unfortunately lends itself to parodies.

'Lloyd George knew my Father' is one of them, and another for the cynics among you:

> 'Like a mighty tortoise
> Moves the Church of God
> Brothers we are treading
> Where we've always trod!'

It's a hymn that is still very popular with brass bands, but think back to when you last sang it in a church service. I've a feeling it won't make the next generation of mainstream hymnbooks, but if Walks of Witness survive into the next century, it may well still serve its original purpose of keeping all of us marching in the right direction.

Left right, left right . . .

Sandy Macpherson, whose programme 'Chapel in the Valley' first introduced Hazel Bradley to the world of hymns.

O WORSHIP THE KING, ALL-GLORIOUS ABOVE
Robert Grant, 1779-1838

O worship the King, all-glorious above;
O gratefully sing his power and his love:
    Our Shield and Defender, the Ancient of Days,
    Pavilioned in splendour, and girded with praise.

O tell of his might, O sing of his grace,
Whose robe is the light, whose canopy space;
    His chariots of wrath the deep thunder-clouds form,
    And dark is his path on the wings of the storm.

The earth with its store of wonders untold,
Almighty, thy power hath founded of old;
    Hath stablished it fast by a changeless decree,
    And round it hath cast, like a mantle, the sea.

Thy bountiful care what tongue can recite?
It breathes in the air, it shines in the light;
    It streams from the hills, it descends to the plain,
    And sweetly distils in the dew and the rain.

Frail children of dust, and feeble as frail,
In thee do we trust, nor find thee to fail;
    Thy mercies how tender, how firm to the end,
    Our Maker, Defender, Redeemer, and Friend.

O measureless Might, ineffable Love,
While angels delight to hymn thee above,
    Thy humbler creation, though feeble their lays,
    With true adoration shall sing to thy praise.

Politicians may have the 'gift of the gab' and be able to craft a clever speech, but hymnwriting is not a skill that would immediately come to mind when you think of your local MP. And yet there have been a number of hymns written by Honourable Members and even one of our Prime Ministers, William Gladstone tried his hand at the art. He wrote 'O lead my blindness by the hand', quite an appropriate request from a politician some might say! But it was the Gladstone bag that caught the imagination of the great British Public rather than his hymns, so you won't find it in many of today's hymnbooks.

I'm afraid the same goes for the works of other notable MPs although I expect some of you will be familiar with the Radical Sir John Bowring's 'In the cross of Christ I glory' and 'For the might of thine arm' written by the Honourable Member for Ipswich, Charles Silvester Horne in 1910. However, 'O worship the King, all glorious above', is the exception. Based on Psalm 104, it is still very popular with preachers who often use it as their first hymn.

The author, Robert Grant, came from a very distinguished line of public servants. One of his ancestors was a soldier killed at Culloden and his father was MP for Inverness, as well as managing a successful business in the East Indies.

Young Robert enjoyed a privileged education and he graduated from Cambridge with flying colours in 1806. The following year he was called to the Bar and his meteoric rise continued when in 1808 he won the Elgin seat for the Tories. In Parliament Robert Grant carried the Bill which emancipated the British Jews.

I suppose that his family connections had something to do with his appointment as Secretary for the Board of Trade for India, yet more distinction beckoned. He was made a Privy Councillor and then offered the position of Governor of Bombay. Fortunately for us he wrote 'O worship the King' just before he went, because he certainly wouldn't have had much time for writing with all the responsibilities that his job entailed.

Throughout his life Robert Grant's Christian principles had been the guiding factor in everything he had undertaken, and just as in Britain he had fought hard for the rights of Jews and many other minority groups, he got down to the task of improving the lot of those who lived in appalling conditions in Bombay. Historians might say that the final accolade came in 1834 when he was honoured with a knighthood, but for those who had benefitted from his passion to relieve suffering, a different tribute seemed more appropriate, and after his premature death at the age of fifty-nine, the people of Bombay built a medical school in his memory, bearing his name. It was left to his brother to publish his hymns, and just a year after Sir Robert's death a collection of twelve became available under the title 'Sacred Poems'.

'O worship the King' was one of them and it has been sung and enjoyed by many people for over one hundred and fifty years.

ROCK OF AGES

Augustus Montague Toplady, 1740-1778

Rock of Ages, cleft for me,
Let me hide myself in thee;
Let the water and the blood,
From thy riven side which flowed,
Be of sin the double cure,
Cleanse me from its guilt and power.

Not the labours of my hands
Can fulfil thy law's demands;
Could my zeal no respite know,
Could my tears for ever flow,
All for sin could not atone:
Thou must save, and thou alone.

Nothing in my hand I bring,
Simply to thy cross I cling;
Naked, come to thee for dress;
Helpless, look to thee for grace;
Foul, I to the fountain fly;
Wash me, Saviour, or I die.

While I draw this fleeting breath,
When mine eyes shall close in death,
When I soar through tracts unknown,
See thee on thy judgement throne,
Rock of Ages, cleft for me,
Let me hide myself in thee.

'At Burrington Combe or not at Burrington Combe?' That is the question, or rather one of the questions that surround the hymn 'Rock of Ages'. But then its author, Augustus Montague Toplady was also something of an enigma and certainly not half as popular as his hymn has become.

He was born in 1740, and never knew his father. It was an uncle who looked after him, sending him to Westminster School where he presumed to lecture everyone through pious sermons, and when that didn't work wrote a farce instead, which he sent to Drury Lane. Uncle was displeased at this development and young Augustus and his mother were moved to Ireland, out of harm's way. There he attended Trinity College in Dublin, and although a member of the Established Church, he was converted to Wesleyanism after attending a service in a barn.

Toplady had caught the religious bug, or rather butterfly, as only a few months after joining his new sect he fluttered into Calvinism and John Wesley was rejected, though not forgotten, as we shall see. He was ordained, and finally took a living in Exeter, where he became rather attached to an historian, Mrs Macaulay who lived in Bath. They corresponded regularly and it looks as though Augustus expected marriage, but his hopes were dashed when the forty-seven year old woman of his dreams married what today we might call a 'toy boy', a very pleasant surgeon's mate who was just twenty-one!

Reverend Toplady was furious and he was not a man to hide his feelings. We only have to read what he wrote about John Wesley. He never forgave the great man for publicly rejecting Calvin's doctrine of the elect, and accused him of coarseness, satanic guilt and shamelessness. All this venom from the same pen that wrote the words of the hymn we love so well!

There are two stories that surround the writing of 'Rock of Ages'. One is that Charles Wesley and Toplady had met and had a heated argument, then each had retired to their room, Wesley to write 'Jesu, lover of my soul', and Toplady to write 'The Rock'. But the other, more popular story concerns a visit to Blagden, where during a storm Augustus sheltered in a cleft rock in the Mendips called Burrington Combe. Not having a notebook in which to write his hymn he found a playing card on the ground and used that.

Somehow a Calvinist and the ace of spades don't quite match and neither, I'm afraid, do these stories. Augustus Toplady would not have even reached the age of one when Charles Wesley wrote his hymn, and when 'Rock of Ages' was published in 1776 the author had not been near the West Country for twelve years. Also, the words look suspiciously like a paragraph that appears in a preface to 'The Hymns on the Lord's Supper', which was published a few years earlier.

However, what we *can* verify is the rider which he added to the hymn when it first appeared in 'Gospel Magazine'. He had calculated that if sins multiplied with every second, at ten years old a boy would be chargeable with three hundred and fifteen million and thirty-six thousand sins. Not the kind of comment that is likely to increase the numbers of children in Sunday School!

Augustus died when he was thirty-eight. Perhaps it is just as well he did not have access to a calculator, but in spite of his dubious life-style, he has left us with a hymn that has inspired, challenged and strengthened many people over the years. And if we want to imagine the events of Burrington Combe, why shouldn't we?

STILL THE NIGHT

Joseph Mohr, 1792-1848

Still the night, holy the night!
Sleeps the world; hid from sight,
Mary and Joseph in stable bare
Watch o'er the child belovèd and fair
    Sleeping in heavenly rest.

Still the night, holy the night!
Shepherds first saw the light,
Heard resounding clear and long,
Far and near, the angel-song:
    'Christ the Redeemer is here!'

Still the night, holy the night!
Son of God, O how bright
Love is smiling from thy face!
Strikes for us now the hour of grace,
    Saviour, since thou art born!

Hickory dickory dock, the mouse ran up the . . . no, not the clock this time, but the organ pipe! The organ in question was in the Church of St Nicholas, Obendorf in the mountains of Austria, and during the night of the 23rd December 1818, the mouse gnawed its way through the bellows, rendering the fine instrument utterly useless.

Imagine the dismay of the young organist Franz Gruber when on Christmas Eve he attempted to practise the hymns for the Midnight Mass. Not a peep to be heard except the scampering of tiny feet.

He was soon joined by the assistant priest, his great friend Joseph Mohr, and together they looked desperately for a solution. The organ couldn't be repaired in time for the midnight service, and the mass without any music just wouldn't be the same, especially on such a special night when the church would be packed. What could they do?

It was then that Joseph pulled out of his pocket a crumpled piece of paper and asked Franz to have a look at what was written on it.

> 'Stille Nacht! Heilige Nacht!'
> 'Still the night! Holy the night!'

It was his latest poem. Perhaps it could be sung with a guitar and just a few voices. What did his friend think?

By all accounts Gruber was more than impressed and set to work to write an accompaniment for the guitar, using children's voices to underline the simplicity of the Nativity scene.

It seemed strange to the villagers as they entered the church a few hours later. There was no organ playing, and although there were the chants, it wasn't the same without the music. But then after the sermon came the surprise. The two young men and twelve children stepped forward and the hymn that has become so much part of our Christmas worship was sung for the very first time.

Like every innovation, it had a mixed reception. Some of the worshippers were appalled by the sound of a guitar on such a sacred occasion, while others found the simple words and haunting tune conjured up an image of the first Christmas that would stay with them for many years. But how did the hymn gain a wider audience?

It's back to the mousehole for the answer, because when the organ repairer finally arrived and heard the story and the hymn, he was so excited by it that he took it to many of the churches he visited and soon it was being sung all over Austria.

It reached Britain in 1858, translated by Emily Eliot for a church choir in Brighton and since then has been translated in many different ways. In some books it is 'Silent Night' in others, 'Still the night'. It is still many people's favourite carol, and to think it all started with a hungry mouse!

TELL ME THE OLD, OLD STORY
Arabella Katherine Hankey, 1834-1911

Tell me the old, old story
    Of unseen things above,
Of Jesus and his glory,
    Of Jesus and his love.
Tell me the story simply,
    As to a little child;
For I am weak, and weary,
    And helpless, and defiled:
        Tell me the old, old story,
        Of Jesus and his love.

Tell me the story slowly,
    That I may take it in –
That wonderful redemption,
    God's remedy for sin.
Tell me the story often,
    For I forget so soon;
The early dew of morning
    Has passed away at noon:

Tell me the story softly,
    With earnest tones and grave;
Remember, I'm the sinner
    Whom Jesus came to save.
Tell me the story always,
    If you would really be
In any time of trouble
    A comforter to me:

Tell me the same old story
    When you have cause to fear
That this world's empty glory
    Is costing me too dear.
And when that next world's glory
    Is dawning on my soul,
Tell me the old, old story –
    Christ Jesus makes thee whole!

It's back to my old haunts for the origin of another popular hymn. I was surprised to find that a house that I walked by in Croydon nearly every day for many years turned out to be the place where the writer of one of our best loved hymns spent her formative years.

'Tell me the old, old story, of Jesus and his love.' This is the chorus, but in fact the author, Katherine Hankey, was very unhappy when her poem appeared bearing this refrain, as she hadn't actually written it! It had been added by the editor without her permission, and she felt it quite spoilt the continuity of the fifty-two verses.

Arabella Katherine Hankey was born in 1834 into a middle class family with a passion for good works. They felt it their Christian duty to preach the gospel to the less fortunate. Her father, a London banker, was a member of the evangelical 'Clapham Sect', and young Katherine followed in his footsteps by starting her own mission to shop girls when she was only eighteen. She would visit all the large West End Stores and personally invite girls to come to a Bible study where she would share with them the 'old, old story'.

I have often found, when looking into the background of hymns, that there are sometimes two or more incidents which lay claim to have been the inspiration behind them, particularly the evangelical ones, and in this case there seem to be two conflicting stories. One source reveals that Miss Hankey heard of an old Irish priest who lay dying. A young minister who was with him was becoming confused in his efforts to communicate the eternal truths, and in desperation the old man cried out:

> 'Just tell me the old, old story . . . that and nothing else.'

And so many would have us believe that it was that cry from the heart that was behind the writing of the hymn.

But the other version of the story reveals that on the 29th January 1886, Katherine Hankey, weak and weary after a long illness, realized that simple thoughts in simple words were all that could be coped with in such a situation. She put pen to paper and wrote a poem entitled 'The story wanted'.

However the hymn came to be written, Messrs Moody and Sankey recognised its potential as a tool for conversion and 'Tell me the old, old story' rang round many revival meetings.

Composer William Doane, who wrote the tune, tells of the day he saw a Major-General reading Miss Hankey's poem with tears streaming down his cheeks and from that moment he knew he must set it to music. Words and music produced an immensely popular hymn, one of those few originating from 'Sacred Songs and Solos' which has survived in our modern hymnbooks. The teachings of the Bible were central to Katherine Hankey and the message of her hymn is a fitting one for today.

'Tell me the story simply, slowly and often'; perhaps the words should be inscribed on every pulpit!

THE CHURCH'S ONE FOUNDATION
Samuel John Stone, 1839-1900

The church's one foundation
    Is Jesus Christ her Lord;
She is his new creation
    By water and the word;
From heaven he came and sought her
    To be his holy bride;
With his own blood he bought her,
    And for her life he died.

Elect from every nation,
    Yet one o'er all the earth,
Her charter of salvation
    One Lord, one faith, one birth;
One holy name she blesses,
    Partakes one holy food,
And to one hope she presses
    With every grace endued.

'Mid toil and tribulation,
    And tumult of her war,
She waits the consummation
    Of peace for evermore;
Till with the vision glorious
    Her longing eyes are blest,
And the great church victorious
    Shall be the church at rest.

Yet she on earth has union
    With God the Three in One,
And mystic sweet communion
    With those whose rest is won.
O happy ones and holy!
    Lord, give us grace that we,
Like them, the meek and lowly,
    On high may dwell with thee.

The reasons for writing hymns are many and varied but surely there cannot be many like 'The Church's one foundation' which was written as the result of an argument! Although certain personalities were very much to the fore, it was not a personal argument, but a theological one.

In the 1980s the Bishop of Durham caused quite a stir in the Church of England when some clergy thought his views on Christ's resurrection didn't concur with some of the articles of the Creed. But back in 1863, Bishop John Colenso of Natal was deposed and excommunicated because of his unorthodox views on the doctrine of eternal punishment, and his suggestion that Moses might not have written the first five books of the Bible. In those days South Africa must have seemed even further away than it does today, but when the news reached Britain it sparked off a tremendous row with some clergy calling Colenso heretic, and others calling for his re-instatement.

One young curate, Samuel John Stone from Windsor, was outraged that a bishop should question what he considered to be the fundamentals of Christian belief, and so he wrote a hymn on each of the twelve articles of the Creed defending the traditional view. The ninth article reads 'I believe in the holy catholic Church, the communion of saints', and it is on this which 'The Church's one foundation' is based.

Of course, it's been chopped, changed and added to over the years, which we have come to expect, but it does seem a pity that the very verse which has the cutting edge, which includes the lines 'By schisms rent asunder, by heresies distrest' is omitted in most modern hymnbooks, although I can see why some people might find it 'unhelpful'.

It's a hymn that is often used on grand occasions, as the tune is one which lends itself to a procession, with its air of stateliness and dignity.

There is a story attached to the naming of the tune, 'Aurelia'. It was composed by Samuel Sebastian Wesley at his home in Winchester for another hymn, 'Jerusalem the Golden', and when he'd finished it he rushed into the drawing room where Mrs Wesley was entertaining some guests, sat down at the piano and played it to the assembled company. His wife immediately christened it 'Aurelia' from the Latin for gold, and Dr Wesley was heard to exclaim, 'I think this will be popular.'

He was absolutely right, although I do think he might have made the last note a little shorter. I always run out of breath before getting to the 'd' in 'Lord'!

THE DAY THOU GAVEST
John Ellerton, 1826-1893

The day thou gavest, Lord, is ended,
    The darkness falls at thy behest;
To thee our morning hymns ascended,
    Thy praise shall sanctify our rest.

We thank thee that thy Church unsleeping,
    While earth rolls onward into light,
Through all the world her watch is keeping,
    And rests not now by day or night.

As o'er each continent and island
    The dawn leads on another day,
The voice of prayer is never silent,
    Nor dies the strain of praise away.

The sun that bids us rest is waking
    Our brethren 'neath the western sky,
And hour by hour fresh lips are making
    Thy wondrous doings heard on high.

So be it, Lord; thy throne shall never,
    Like earth's proud empires, pass away;
Thy kingdom stands, and grows for ever,
    Till all thy creatures own thy sway.

'The day thou gavest, Lord, is ended' has been in the Top Ten of Hymns for over one hundred and sixteen years! The author, the Reverend John Ellerton, was born in London but, as usual for the middle-class twelve year olds of nineteenth century Britain, he was sent away to be educated, to King William's College on the Isle of Man. There is a rumour that he was quite glad to get away as his mother wrote short stories of the moral kind, and what teenage boy wants to be associated with titles such as, 'How little Fanny learned to be useful'! Unfortunately, while he was away, first his father then his brother died, and so in 1844 when his mother moved to Ulverston on the Lancashire coast he had no option but to go with her. But not for long, as he continued his education at Cambridge University and was ordained in 1850.

After a short spell in Sussex where he was married, he moved back up North and took an incumbency in Cheshire. Mother came too, and you can see her grave today in the village of Crewe Green where John Ellerton had the care of the farmers and the workers on the estate owned by the Marquis of Crewe. He also had the pastoral care of the men and boys at the London North Western Railway works. This was to be the busiest time of his life, and yet it was at Crewe Green that he wrote most of his finest hymns, including 'Saviour, again to thy dear name we raise', which was written especially for a Festival of Parish Choirs in Nantwich.

'The day thou gavest' is also from this period and it appears that Reverend Ellerton saw the first line in an anonymous hymn, liked it, and used it as the beginning of a hymn which was to be included in a Liturgy for missionary meetings.

It was first published in a revised version of Church Hymns in 1874 and shortly afterwards John was invited to submit that one and others for entry into 'Hymns Ancient and Modern'. He spent more and more time on his hymns and hymnology generally, and by the time he left the North to go back to London he was generally thought of as something of an expert in this field.

St Mary's Barnes in London, however, was to leave him with sad memories. Three of his children died while they were there and John himself became ill with pleurisy. So it was in the countryside of Essex that John Ellerton spent his final days, but if you want to visit his final resting place you will have to go to Torquay as he died while convalescing and is buried there. What a pity that he didn't live for just four more years, because then he could have heard 'The day thou gavest, Lord, is ended' sung in churches up and down the country in celebration of Queen Victoria's Diamond Jubilee. The old lady had chosen it herself as it was one of her particular favourites.

It was also the favourite of Bill Pearson who was our church organist for many years, and when the congregation saw number 667 (Methodist Hymn Book) up on the hymn board we all knew that the service would be concluding with pedals pounding and all stops pulled out!

THE KING OF LOVE
Henry Williams Baker, 1821-1877

The King of love my Shepherd is,
    Whose goodness faileth never;
I nothing lack if I am his
    And he is mine for ever.

Where streams of living water flow
    My ransomed soul he leadeth,
And where the verdant pastures grow
    With food celestial feedeth.

Perverse and foolish oft I strayed,
    But yet in love he sought me,
And on his shoulder gently laid,
    And home rejoicing brought me.

In death's dark vale I fear no ill
    With thee, dear Lord, beside me;
Thy rod and staff my comfort still,
    Thy cross before to guide me.

Thou spread'st a table in my sight;
    Thy unction grace bestoweth;
And O what transport of delight
    From thy pure chalice floweth!

And so through all the length of days
    Thy goodness faileth never:
Good Shepherd, may I sing thy praise
    Within thy house for ever.

There are some hymns which seem to be appropriate for every occasion, and 'The King of Love my Shepherd is' is one that definitely falls into that category. You may have chosen it for your wedding, your confirmation, your child's baptism or possibly sung it at a loved one's funeral. It is a classic among hymns, first appearing in the Appendix to the 1868 'Hymns Ancient and Modern'. Its author, Sir Henry Williams Baker, was one of the editors of that book which was one of the milestones in English hymnody.

The son of a Vice-Admiral, graduate of Trinity College, Cambridge, ordained in 1844, and titled seven years later, you might imagine Henry Williams Baker as the leading light of a prestigious city parish, but you would be wrong. He spent twenty-five years of his life in the small village of Monkland situated on the English-Welsh border in Herefordshire.

It was an idyllic existence, as Sir Henry's parish duties were hardly demanding, and although he may have regretted the fact that family life had passed him by, he had plenty of time to spend on his writing. One of his books is entitled, 'Daily prayers for those who have to work hard'. I think it was aimed at the farm labourers he saw day after day, working long hours in all weathers with no respite.

But although he lived in this backwater, Sir Henry worked tirelessly in the mainstream to produce a hymnbook for the Anglican Church that would have as wide an appeal as possible. It took seventeen years to complete, and its impact was tremendous when the two hundred and seventy-three hymns reached the Church in 1861.

'The King of Love' is based on the 23rd Psalm, and is in all probability a remake of George Herbert's version 'The God of Love' with a different metre, but next time you sing it look at the third verse. Although the imagery of the shepherd reflects the Old Testament psalm, the words, 'And on his shoulder gently laid, and home rejoicing brought me', is very reminiscent of Jesus' parable of the Lost Sheep.

I find it a comforting and reassuring picture, and I was not a bit surprised to find that these were the last words that Henry Williams Baker uttered before he died. Out of the hundreds of hymns that he must have studied while compiling 'Hymns Ancient and Modern', this was the verse that stuck in his mind.

We all know the difference the tune makes to a hymn, and J. B. Dykes' beautiful melody, written especially for the hymn, complements it in every way. Even Vaughan Williams singled it out for special praise.

Henry Williams Baker was only fifty-six when he died, and if you are ever near the village of Monkland, stop and visit the church. You will find that the lych-gate is dedicated to his memory and his grave is nearby.

THOU WHOSE ALMIGHTY WORD
John Marriott, 1780-1825

Thou whose almighty word
Chaos and darkness heard,
   And took their flight,
Hear us, we humbly pray,
And where the gospel day
Sheds not its glorious ray
   Let there be light!

Thou who didst come to bring
On thy redeeming wing
   Healing and sight,
Health to the sick in mind,
Sight to the inly blind,
O now to all mankind
   Let there be light!

Spirit of truth and love,
Life-giving, holy Dove,
   Speed forth thy flight:
Move on the water's face,
Spreading the beams of grace,
And in earth's darkest place
   Let there be light!

Blessèd and holy Three,
Glorious Trinity,
   Grace, love, and might,
Boundless as ocean's tide
Rolling in fullest pride,
Through the world far and wide
   Let there be light!

I always find it difficult to choose hymns for a service on Remembrance Sunday. People come to worship with such different memories and needs. Should I include ones with militaristic images, or deal specifically with death, or are openly patriotic? Am I going to upset certain members of the congregation if I don't include 'O God, our help in ages past'?

One hymn that I do find myself coming back to year after year is 'Thou whose almighty word', based on the opening words in the Genesis creation story: 'Let there be light'.

The author, John Marriott, was born in 1780, and followed exactly the same path as so many of the other hymnwriters of the period. Public school, in this case Rugby, Oxford University and then ordination. There was no shortage of men of the cloth in those days, but a veritable assembly line!

John Marriott was the 1804 model and was immediately snapped up by the Duke of Buccleuch to be the family chaplain and private tutor to his eldest son in Dalkeith Palace in Scotland.

Here he met Sir Walter Scott, and finding they both had a love of literature, they became firm friends, no doubt reading each other's efforts because John actually contributed to one of Scott's publications. But this idyllic period of his life was to be shortlived as his young pupil George became ill and died at the age of just ten years. John himself suffered from very poor health, as did his wife, and they spent some time on the Devonshire coast convalescing from one ailment or another, until John was finally diagnosed as suffering from ossification of the brain.

He only wrote a few hymns and of these only one is sung today but it's still in most of the mainstream hymnbooks although there are two versions of the first line. I know it as 'Thou whose almighty word, chaos and darkness heard', but it could read 'Thou whose eternal word' in your hymnbook, and that actually seems to be the original.

None of John Marriott's hymns were published in his lifetime, not because people didn't want to sing them but because the author was too modest to let them. But within six days of his death in 1825 the Reverend Thomas Mortimer got hold of a copy of 'Thou whose almighty word' and used it at a meeting of the London Missionary Society in Great Queen Street Chapel. How's that for being quick off the mark!

The hymn was published in two hymn books before the year was out and it became very popular indeed, especially as it was sung to the tune of the National Anthem. We use a different tune these days. The editors of 'Hymns Ancient and Modern' didn't think it was quite appropriate and adopted the tune Moscow, so named because its composer F. Giardini, died there.

So why this hymn for Remembrance Sunday? Well, what could be more relevant than a prayer for God's wisdom, love and might to be boundless as ocean's tide and that through the whole world far and wide these words should ring out: 'Let there be light!'

TO GOD BE THE GLORY
Frances Jane van Alstyne, 1820-1915

To God be the glory, great things he has done!
So loved he the world that he gave us his Son,
Who yielded his life in atonement for sin,
And opened the life-gate that all may go in:

Praise the Lord! Praise the Lord!
Let the earth hear his voice!
Praise the Lord! Praise the Lord!
Let the people rejoice!
O come to the Father, through Jesus the Son;
And give him the glory – great things he has done!

O perfect redemption, the purchase of blood,
To every believer the promise of God!
And every offender who truly believes,
That moment from Jesus a pardon receives:

Great things he has taught us, great things he has done,
And great our rejoicing through Jesus the Son;
But purer, and higher, and greater will be
Our wonder, our rapture, when Jesus we see:

If you like a good rousing chorus then the hymn 'To God be the glory' will almost certainly be one of your favourites! It is just one of the eight thousand hymns and sacred songs which flowed from the pen of a prolific American writer, Fanny Crosby. Apparently she had a contract with her publishers to write at least three hymns a week, and used no less than two hundred and sixteen different pen names.

Add to that the fact that in 1820, when she was six weeks old, an incompetent surgeon left her blind and we begin to get the picture of a very determined and hardworking woman.

She lived in New York and attended the Institute for the Blind where her teachers showed very little interest in her verse writing until an itinerant phrenologist 'read her bumps' and declared that she should develop her skill to the full.

She certainly did that and although the 'Mills and Boon of hymnwriters' is rather an unkind title, she certainly could churn them out! Seven or eight hymns a day was nothing to Fanny Crosby.

She also managed to fit in teaching, lecturing and politics – she spoke several times to both Houses of Congress – and also found time to court Alexander van Alstyne and eventually marry him! There are many favourites among her collection of hymns: 'Blessed assurance', 'Rescue the perishing' and 'Safe in the arms of Jesus', which, incidentally, was written in fifteen minutes. They are emotional hymns, used many times by the evangelists Moody and Sankey.

'To God be the glory' was immensely popular with another great evangelist, Billy Graham. In the 1954 London Crusade it became something of a theme song which echoed around the Haringey arena every night.

The tune was written for the hymn by a cloth manufacturer and Sunday School superintendent, one William Doane. He was not quite in the same league as Fanny Crosby, with just a mere two thousand hymn tunes to his credit, but they have both made their mark on hymnbooks all over the world. I'm told that in parts of the USA, there is a special 'Fanny Crosby Day' each year dedicated to her memory, and I've often thought that attempting to sing as many of her songs on that day would make a good sponsored event for a local cause. Although, like Fanny herself, you would need some stamina!

TURN BACK, O MAN
Clifford Bax, 1886-1962

Turn back, O man, forswear thy foolish ways;
Old now is earth, and none may count her days,
Yet thou, her child, whose head is crowned with flame,
Still wilt not hear thine inner God proclaim:
Turn back, O man, forswear thy foolish ways.

Earth might be fair and all men glad and wise,
Age after age their tragic empires rise,
Built while they dream, and in that dreaming weep:
Would man but wake from out his haunted sleep,
Earth might be fair and all men glad and wise.

Earth shall be fair, and all her people one:
Nor till that hour shall God's whole will be done;
Now, even now, once more from earth to sky,
Peals forth in joy man's old undaunted cry:
Earth shall be fair, and all her folk be one.

'Turn back, O man' may not qualify as a 'favourite hymn'; in fact you'd be hard pressed to find it in a modern hymnbook, but strangely enough it has found fame, albeit through a very different channel. If you have seen the rock musical 'Godspell', you may remember the rather surprising opening to the second half of the show. As you listen to the introduction to 'Turn back, O man' it sounds something like the accompaniment to a striptease, and as the singer sits seductively on the lap of some unsuspecting man in the audience and then sidles up on to the stage, you think you could be right!

What Clifford Bax, the author of the hymn, would have made of it, we shall never know. I should imagine that his brother, the celebrated composer Sir Arnold Bax, would have shuddered. Clifford doesn't even get a mention on the 'Godspell' sheet music or the album, but he wasn't around to complain. He died in 1962, just ten years before the musical became a success.

He had what could be described as a privileged life at the turn of the century, attending a private school, and then going on to study art at the Slade. After finishing his course he spent some time on the Continent, gaining valuable experience which he used in the many poems, short stories and plays that he wrote on his return.

In 1942 Clifford's brother, Sir Arnold Bax, was made Master of the King's Music, and his symphonies and works like 'Tintagel' are still popular today. The family had many friends in the worlds of theatre and music, and it was Gustav Holst who in 1916 asked Clifford Bax to write a hymn for an arrangement of the Old 124th from the Geneva Psalter of 1551. The words he wrote reflect what so many people were feeling in the aftermath of the First World War. Losses had been heavy and there was an air of incredulity that such an event could have been allowed to happen, yet in people's minds it was the 'war to end all wars'. Despair was turning to hope, and people felt that better times would return.

>'Earth shall be fair, and all her folk be one.'

The hymn was published in the 'Motherland Song Book' and almost adopted by the League of Nations, since it was sung so often there.

WE PLOUGH THE FIELDS
Matthias Claudius, 1740-1815

We plough the fields, and scatter
    The good seed on the land,
But it is fed and watered
    By God's almighty hand;
He sends the snow in winter,
    The warmth to swell the grain,
The breezes and the sunshine,
    And soft refreshing rain:

    All good gifts around us
        Are sent from heaven above;
    Then thank the Lord, O thank the Lord,
        For all his love.

He only is the maker
    Of all things near and far;
He paints the wayside flower,
    He lights the evening star;
The winds and waves obey him,
    By him the birds are fed;
Much more to us, his children,
    He gives our daily bread:

We thank thee then, O Father,
    For all things bright and good:
The seed-time and the harvest,
    Our life, our health, our food.
Accept the gifts we offer
    For all thy love imparts,
And, what thou most desirest,
    Our humble, thankful hearts:

"Oh good!" I heard someone exclaim as they entered the church and saw the display of fruit and vegetables at the front. "It's harvest. At least I shall know all the hymns!" I smiled because I knew there would be at least two that would be unfamiliar and one that would be conspicuous by its absence.

'We plough the fields, and scatter the good seed on the land.' It used to be a must, sung lustily by adults and children alike, but dare I say, it has waned in popularity of late and these days has been superseded in many church and school festivals by hymns and songs with more modern appeal and relevance.

But we cannot get away from the fact that it has been a harvest favourite for many years and has gone through a few changes too. It started life in 1782 in a German musical. Matthias Claudius, its author, had been brought up by Lutheran parents but when he went to University to study theology he met some of the new free thinkers of that time and became an atheist. He changed his course to law and languages and ended up as a journalist and occasional poet, but in 1777 he became very ill and his old faith returned. Health restored he took on a new job and it's at this point that we begin to see the connection with the hymn because his new post was Commissioner for Agriculture.

Not content with the day-to-day duties that such responsibility brought, Matthias Claudius decided to bring another kind of culture to the people. He wrote a play about a harvest festival in a North German farmhouse which included a song based on one he'd heard sung by some of the peasants as they worked in the fields. There were seventeen verses with a chorus in between, which the publisher obviously thought was a little excessive when it was included in a collection of songs for schools. Six verses only appeared with the chorus and it was this version that a certain Miss Jane Montgomery Campbell espied in 1861 as she was looking for children's hymns to include in a publication entitled 'Garland of Song'. Jane was a Victorian maiden lady living in North Devon who devoted her life to music and children, but at the age of sixty-one she was tragically killed in a carriage accident on Dartmoor.

But the hymn she so enjoyed teaching the children lived on and the editors of 'Hymns Ancient and Modern' altered just two lines before it was given the thumbs up for general use in the Anglican Church. And wasn't it well used!

Every harvest out it came, because for many years there were really only a few hymns written especially for this season. These days there are a variety to choose from dealing with the wider world and issues of poverty and hunger, and yet 'We plough the fields' still remains a firm favourite in many communities.

WHAT A FRIEND WE HAVE IN JESUS
Joseph Medlicott Scriven, 1820-1886

What a friend we have in Jesus,
    All our sins and griefs to bear!
What a privilege to carry
    Everything to God in prayer!
O what peace we often forfeit,
    O what needless pain we bear,
All because we do not carry
    Everything to God in prayer!

Have we trials and temptations,
    Is there trouble anywhere?
We should never be discouraged:
    Take it to the Lord in prayer.
Can we find a friend so faithful
    Who will all our sorrows share?
Jesus knows our every weakness:
    Take it to the Lord in prayer.

Are we weak and heavy laden,
    Cumbered with a load of care?
Precious Saviour, still our refuge –
    Take it to the Lord in prayer!
Do thy friends despise, forsake thee?
    Take it to the Lord in prayer;
In his arms he'll take and shield thee,
    Thou wilt find a solace there.

I can see my grandmother sitting at the piano on a Sunday evening playing her favourite hymns: 'Hold the fort for I am coming' and 'Shall we gather at the river?' There was even one called 'Out of the ark', and you may well be thinking that all those sort of hymns come into that category. 'Nanny Seaford', as she was known, could not read a note of music, she played by ear, but the book from which all the hymns came still stood proudly in front of her. 'Sacred Songs and Solos', compiled and sung by Ira D. Sankey.

Put that name alongside Dwight L. Moody and we have the American partnership which created the gospel hymn. Words that could overwhelm you with guilt: 'Will you be there?', 'Will your anchor hold?', 'Almost persuaded'. There were some that were a little more positive and talked of sins forgiven and prayers answered, and one of these has become a great favourite:

> 'What a friend we have in Jesus,
> All our sins and griefs to bear'.

Its Irish author, Joseph Medlicott Scriven, knew all about grief and wrote from bitter experience. As a boy he desperately wanted a military career, but his health let him down. As a young man he met the woman he wanted to make his wife, but tragically she was drowned on the eve of the wedding. So in 1845 he packed up and emigrated to Canada, hoping that a new land with new opportunities would allow him to make a fresh start, but it wasn't to be. At first he seemed to do well, gaining a position as a tutor and finding another girl, but once again tragedy struck and she too died just before the wedding. Joseph Scriven never really recovered from the shock, and sadly, in 1886, he was found drowned in a water-run by Lake Rice. Just before his death, a neighbour, tidying his room, came across a manuscript containing the words of our hymn, and Joseph had explained that 'he and the Lord had written it between them' to comfort his mother when she was going through a particular time of sorrow.

As far as we know these were the only verses he wrote, but they so impressed Mr Sankey that he included them in his very first edition of 'Gospel Hymns'. 'What a friend we have in Jesus' has been well-loved by many other people too, and when there was talk of leaving it out of the Methodist 'Hymns and Psalms', there was uproar in some circles and it just had to be included.

Like so many hymns a particular tune has become welded to Scriven's words, and is so special to many Christians that when they heard it used in a television commercial for a certain make of car, complaints were sent to the Advertising Standards Body in an attempt to have it removed from our screens. I don't remember there being much of a fuss, however, when it was parodied in the film 'O, what a lovely war'.

Disappointment, sorrow and grief play a part in the lives of everyone, and yet this hymn speaks of peace, refuge and solace. Whenever I include it in a service it is plainly a popular choice and as I sing it I remember my grandmother playing the piano. No doubt the members of the congregation are conjuring up all their memories too.

WHEN THE ROLL IS CALLED UP YONDER
James Milton Black, 1856-1938

When the trumpet of the Lord shall sound, and time shall be no more,
    And the morning breaks, eternal, bright and fair,
When the saved of earth shall gather over on the other shore,
    And the roll is called up yonder, I'll be there.

    When the roll is called up yonder, I'll be there.

On that bright and cloudless morning, when the dead in Christ shall rise,
    And the glory of his resurrection share,
When his chosen ones shall gather to their home beyond the skies,
    And the roll is called up yonder, I'll be there.

Let us labour for the Master from the dawn till setting sun
    Let us tell of all his wondrous love and care;
Then, when all of life is over, and our work on earth is done,
    And the roll is called up yonder, we'll be there.

A shrinking violet is most definitely *not* the phrase that one could use to describe the author of 'When the roll is called up yonder'. In one of his letters dated 1913, he refers to it as the greatest song that had been written for the last twenty-five years!

James Milton Black was an American Methodist, a musician who taught singing and wrote hymns which were very popular and published in various gospel song-books. 'When the roll is called up yonder' was included in one of his own collections called 'Songs of the soul' and fortunately for us he wrote an account of its origin:

> 'One day I met a girl, fourteen years old, poorly clad and a child of a drunkard. She accepted my invitation to attend Sunday School and one evening at a consecration meeting when members answered the roll call by repeating scripture texts, she failed to respond. I spoke of what a sad thing it would be when our names are called from the Lamb's book of life, if one of us should be absent. I longed for something suitable to sing just then, but I could find nothing in the books. We closed the service, and on my way home the thought came to me "Why don't you make it?" I dismissed the idea thinking that I could never write such a hymn. When I reached my home my wife saw that I was deeply troubled and questioned me, but I made no reply. Then the words in the first stanza came to me in full. In fifteen minutes more I had composed the other two verses. Going to the piano I played the music, just as it is found today in the hymnbooks, and I have never dared to change a single word or note of the music since.'

The fact that the girl who inspired the hymn died from pneumonia shortly after added an emotional dimension and its popularity grew, so much so that James Black felt able to make the claim that it had gone into more books than any other one gospel song in the English language, and therefore justified his inclusion price of twenty-five dollars.

Perhaps later editors didn't think it worth the money as it's not in many of our modern hymnbooks. It does sound very dated and extremely repetitive, but it's still a favourite with many people.

I remember playing it on the piano from an old Billy Graham song-book which belonged to my father's Gospel Male Voice Choir, and as it was easy to play and my sight reading was poor, I could pick out the right hand and vamp away with the left. My father tells me his choir still sings it by popular request!

WHEN WE WALK WITH THE LORD
John Henry Sammis, 1846-1919

When we walk with the Lord
In the light of his word,
What a glory he sheds on our way!
While we do his good will,
He abides with us still,
And with all who will trust and obey:

Trust and obey, for there's no other way
To be happy in Jesus,
But to trust and obey.

Not a burden we bear,
Not a sorrow we share,
But our toil he doth richly repay;
Not a grief nor a loss,
Not a frown nor a cross,
But is blest if we trust and obey:

But we never can prove
The delights of his love
Until all on the altar we lay:
For the favour he shows,
And the joy he bestows,
Are for them who will trust and obey:

Then in fellowship sweet
We will sit at his feet,
Or we'll walk by his side in the way;
What he says we will do,
Where he sends we will go –
Never fear, only trust and obey:

'When we walk with the Lord' is one of those hymns which are known not by the first line of the first verse but by the first line of the chorus, in this case 'Trust and Obey'. In fact sometimes it's a struggle to remember the beginning of the hymn because it's the chorus that sticks in the mind.

When I was in Sunday School we used to have a 'chorus time' using the CSSM book where we'd shout out the numbers of the ones we wanted to sing. If we didn't like the speaker who had been invited to 'give the word' we were very naughty and kept begging our leader for more of our favourite choruses so that the poor visitor only had a few minutes in which to bore us! I became very familiar with choruses like 'In my heart there rings a melody' and 'Turn your eyes upon Jesus' but at the time I had no idea that many of them were choruses to hymns included in the Moody and Sankey collections. 'When we walk with the Lord' is from an edition of their 'Sacred Songs and Solos'.

Strangely, the inspiration for the hymn came from the composer of the tune, Mr Daniel Towner. He worked for Dwight Moody in his Chicago Bible Institute, training people in the noble art of songleading for the great evangelical campaigns.

At one of these meetings in Massachusetts when Daniel Towner himself was singing and conducting the audience, a young man stood up and shouted out, 'I am not quite sure, but I am going to trust and I am going to obey.' It had to be a cue for a song and the songleader didn't miss it!

He jotted the sentence down and sent it to John H. Sammis, a successful businessman who had given up his career to take up a full time appointment with the YMCA. He was fascinated by the story and wrote these now familiar lines:

> 'Trust and obey, for there's no other way
> To be happy in Jesus, but to trust and obey.'

So with this hymn it was the chorus that came first and it was later that the author developed the five verses which outline more fully the various aspects of life that the Christian must commit to God in order to gain lasting happiness.

Daniel Towner then completed the tune we know so well and the words and music became inseparable. The hymn was published in 1887 and immediately became a very popular choice in those American Revival meetings. In Britain, as 'Moody Mania' began to take hold, British song leaders carried on the tradition, and 'Trust and Obey' was always a great favourite and easy to learn.

Whether that young man who'd been its inspiration was ever aware that his words had been immortalised we don't know. But it would be nice to think that the trust and obedience he promised that night brought him the certainty and happiness he was looking for.

WHILE SHEPHERDS WATCHED
Nahum Tate, 1652-1715

While shepherds watched their flocks by night,
    All seated on the ground,
The angel of the Lord came down,
    And glory shone around.

'Fear not,' said he (for mighty dread
    Had seized their troubled mind),
'Glad tidings of great joy I bring
    To you and all mankind.

'To you in David's town this day
    Is born of David's line
A Saviour, who is Christ the Lord;
    And this shall be the sign:

'The heavenly Babe you there shall find
    To human view displayed,
All meanly wrapped in swaddling bands,
    And in a manger laid.'

Thus spake the seraph; and forthwith
    Appeared a shining throng
Of angels praising God, and thus
    Addressed their joyful song:

'All glory be to God on high,
    And to the earth be peace;
Goodwill henceforth from heaven to men
    Begin and never cease.'

Nahum. A good old Biblical name for the author of a good old Biblical hymn that must surely be among the most well-known if not the most well-loved of our Christmas carols, 'While shepherds watched their flocks by night'.

Nahum Tate was the Poet Laureate of 1692 and although I doubt that this was his finest work, these six verses have certainly stood the test of time. Everybody knows this carol, and I couldn't begin to recount the number of parodies that have grown up over the years. If you are still singing about washing socks around a tub you're decades out of date!

I don't know whether Nahum Tate had a sense of humour. His father was an Irish clergyman who'd written a few poems, so perhaps this was what kindled his own interest. He was a clever boy, who graduated from Trinity College, Dublin, and then looked for work in England.

Here he met up with a rather notorious playwright John Dryden, who'd just written the first part of a controversial poem 'Absalom and Ahithophel'. The second part was still only in draft form when he had to start on another play and so Nahum finished it off for him.

Shakespeare may have been interested to read Tate's re-write of 'King Lear' with a 'happy ever after' ending, but eventually he gained the confidence to write some plays of his own. Perhaps his most famous work is the libretto of Purcell's 'Dido and Aeneas' but I like the sound of his chief original poem which has the fascinating title 'Panacea – a poem on Tea'.

It's rather a pity that he didn't stick to tea, because his liking of more than just a drop of 'the hard stuff' led to his downfall. He spent more and more of his money on alcohol and fell deeper and deeper into debt. From a man who had been described as 'good natured but fuddling' he now became 'intemperate and improvident' and he saw out his last days in a refuge for debtors.

In his better days he had published 'A new version of the psalms of David', working with a fellow Irishman Nicholas Brady. The other famous hymn which he wrote was 'Through all the changing scenes of life', and you may also know 'As pants the hart for cooling streams'.

'While shepherds watched' is a paraphrase of Luke 2:8-14, and it first appeared in a supplement to Tate's psalm book in 1700, along with five other hymns, two for Easter and three for Communion.

For most people there is only one tune and that's Winchester Old, but its association with this hymn only goes back to 1861, although the tune itself is much older. Then there's the one with the chorus of 'Sweet chiming Christmas bells', a favourite with American congregations, but I have to say that my favourite tune is Lyngham – as long as you've got some good basses and tenors in the congregation!

WHOSOEVER HEARETH! SHOUT, SHOUT THE SOUND
Philipp Bliss, 1838-1876

Whosoever heareth! Shout, shout the sound;
Send the blessèd tidings all the world around;
Spread the joyful news wherever man is found:
   Whosoever will may come.

>*Whosoever will! Whosoever will!*
>*Send the proclamation over vale and hill;*
>*'Tis the loving Father calls the wanderer home;*
>*Whosoever will may come.*

Whosoever cometh need not delay;
Now the door is open, enter while you may;
Jesus is the true and only living Way:
   Whosoever will may come.

Whosoever will, the promise is secure;
Whosoever will, for ever shall endure;
Whosoever will, 'tis life for evermore;
   Whosoever will may come.

I thought it was a printing error at first. Philipp with two p's at the end? But I was wrong. Mrs Bliss had intended her son's name to be spelt in that way and what's more his middle name began with P too, and so in true American style he was affectionately known to his friends as PP!

He started life in a backwater of Pennsylvania in 1838 and was brought up as a Methodist, but on moving to Chicago, the choir of the newly formed Congregational Church lured him away, as he was no mean singer and delighted in the Psalms and other musical settings of Scripture verses. He found a job with a music company, representing them at various Conventions and Institutes, and it was at one of these jamborees that he met Dwight Moody, the celebrated evangelist.

Dwight was always on the look out for new talent and invited Philipp to sing at one of his Campaign meetings. He was a huge success. People flocked down to the front to be saved when he was singing, and as he increasingly turned his hand to his own songs, he found himself being drawn more and more on to the Moody and Sankey platform. All royalties were ploughed back into the cause and his collection entitled 'Gospel Songs' was a best seller. This has been the name by which all songs of this style have been known ever since and Philipp Bliss is often referred to as the 'Father of Gospel Music'. He liked to write about topical events: the sinking of a boat in Cleveland harbour inspired 'Let the lower lights be burning'. But he also turned to history for his inspiration. It was as hope was running out at a beseiged Unionist depot that the message was flagged 'Hold the fort for I am coming', and that hymn was immensely popular when Moody and Sankey arrived in Britain.

'Whosoever heareth' was written as a result of a sermon given by an English boy in Chicago who Mr Moody originally thought too young to preach. It seems that he preached on John 3:16 every night for seven nights and by the end of the week people were impressed with what the young man had to say. The outcome was this hymn which is more often referred to as 'Whosoever will'.

In 1876 Philipp and his wife were returning home after spending Christmas with their family at home when their train crashed. It burst into flames and Philipp managed to jump clear. He looked round for his wife but she was still trapped in the burning wreckage, and so without any hesitation he went back in and struggled to free her, but they both died in the intense heat.

An untimely death, but as one hymnologist wrote, 'It was not a tragic death, let us look on it rather as a noble one.'

WHO WOULD TRUE VALOUR SEE
John Bunyan, 1628-1688

Who would true valour see,
    Let him come hither;
One here will constant be,
    Come wind, come weather;
There's no discouragement
Shall make him once relent
His first avowed intent
    To be a pilgrim.

Whoso beset him round
    With dismal stories
Do but themselves confound;
    His strength the more is.
No lion can him fright;
He'll with a giant fight;
But he will have a right
    To be a pilgrim.

Hobgoblin nor foul fiend
    Can daunt his spirit;
He knows he at the end
    Shall life inherit.
Then fancies fly away,
He'll fear not what men say;
He'll labour night and day
    To be a pilgrim.

'A godless youth, a liar, a cheat, and a blasphemer to boot.' This is how John Bunyan described himself, as a young man living first on his wits as a tinker and then joining up as a soldier in the Civil War of 1642.

Perhaps it was the sights of war he witnessed that changed him, but it was 'Holy John Gifford', the pastor of the Elstow Congregational Church who later guided him towards writing and preaching.

Not that he needed much pushing. He was an explosive character. You wouldn't forget his sermons in a hurry, and neither did the authorities, because 'Bishop Bunyan' as he called himself, was not ordained and did not hold a preaching licence. He got away with it for a while but was eventually arrested and thrown into Bedford Gaol.

I don't know whether his gaoler respected or feared his charge, but John was allowed all sorts of privileges until someone discovered what was going on, and then the loyal Mrs Bunyan had to be content with pushing jugs of soup through the bars and receiving in exchange the shoelaces her husband had been taught to make, the sale of which would keep the wolf from her door.

John was in prison for a total of twelve years, and it was during this final spell of incarceration that he wrote the work that was to ensure his place in the history of English literature, 'Pilgrim's Progress', 'the journey of a Christian soul.'

I doubt that this book features in today's GCSE English syllabus, but characters like Mr Valiant-for-the-truth still stick in my mind from childhood days. I had a beautifully illustrated copy of the book and I used to turn time and time again to the picture of a radiant Christian at the Cross with his burden tumbling down the hill. It is that image which is conjured up every time I sing the hymn, 'Who would true valour see'. Of course, this song comes much earlier in the book, after a conversation with Mr Greatheart, and although John Bunyan always felt that his poetry was a little primitive, these verses have stood the test of time and still appear in our modern hymnbooks.

You may have noticed that there is a different version of the hymn which begins, 'He who would valiant be', this being a version written by Percy Dearmer in 1906. He must have taken offence at the reference to 'hobgoblins and foul fiends' because these mysteriously disappear. The editors of the English Hymnal liked it and included it in their collection, but most have kept to the original.

We wouldn't dream of singing it to any other tune than Vaughan Williams' Monk's Gate, and there is an interesting story behind that. Apparently the composer first heard it played by a collector of old folk tunes. He was told that it dated back to the time of John Bunyan and was called 'Welcome Sailor'. Strangely enough the metre of Bunyan's poem is exactly the same as many of the ballads of his time including one called 'The valiant sailor's happy return'. So it could be that we sing the tune that inspired John Bunyan as he sat in his prison cell. It's an interesting thought.

INDEX OF AUTHORS

Adams, Sarah Flower	48	Oxenham, John	36
Alexander, Cecil Frances	8		
Alford, Henry	18	Rossetti, Christina Georgina	38
Alstyne, Frances Jane van	76		
		Sammis, John Henry	86
Baker, Henry Williams	72	Scriven, Joseph Medlicott	82
Baring-Gould, Sabine	56	Sears, Edmund Hamilton	40
Bax, Clifford	78	Stone, Samuel John	68
Black, James Milton	84		
Bliss, Philipp	90	Tate, Nahum	88
Boberg, Carl	34	Thring, Godfrey	20
Bode, John Ernest	54	Toplady, Augustus Montague	62
Bridges, Matthew	20		
Bunyan, John	92	Watts, Isaac	52
Byrom, John	16	Wesley, Charles	12
		Whiting, William	24
Claudius, Matthias	80	Whittier, John Greenleaf	22
		Williams, William	28
Doddridge, Philip	30		
Edmeston, James	44		
Ellerton, John	70		
Grant, Robert	60		
Green, Fred Pratt	42		
Hankey, Arabella Katherine	66		
Heber, Reginald	32		
How, William Walsham	26		
Howe, Julia Ward	46		
Lyte, Henry Francis	6		
Marriott, John	74		
Mohr, Joseph	64		
Neale, John Mason (tr.)	50		
Newton, John	10		
Noel, Caroline Maria	14		